MY LIFE WITH KARMA

MY LIFE WITH KARMA

TRAVIS SACKETT

NEW DEGREE PRESS

MY LIFE WITH KARMA

ISBN   978-1-63730-454-9 *Paperback*
            978-1-63730-565-2 *Kindle Ebook*
            978-1-63730-566-9 *Ebook*

TABLE OF CONTENTS

——————

AUTHOR'S NOTE

————

A year has gone by since I lost my best friend. Two hospital stays, a memorial tattoo, and a sea of antipsychotics later, I still feel as heartbroken as the day she passed. After sitting with my pain and realizing modern medicine has no cure for my affliction, I decided to write the story of the rescue dog that rescued me.

My story starts before all of that, however. It details how I've lived as both a drug addict and a police officer. Many believe that drug addicts willingly choose their lifestyle, and that all police officers are innately racists. Neither of these viewpoints is true.

I became addicted to Oxycontin after suffering a back injury. It is now a commonly held belief that the manufacturers of this drug knew that it was highly addictive, but at the time, I never thought that taking a drug prescribed by a doctor would nearly destroy my life.

Furthermore, I can undoubtedly state that I never woke up yearning to become an addict or thief. Instead, chemical changes to my brain chemistry, coupled with an undiagnosed mental health condition, turned me into someone incapable of loving anything more than a pill.

When I was without my drug of choice, my thoughts and cravings solely revolved around when and how I would obtain my next fix. Alcohol intermittently served as an inadequate substitute once I was no longer using opioids. Cross addiction kept me locked in a cycle of addictive and potentially deadly behaviors.

Approximately 130 people die per day in the United States after overdosing on opioids, according to Centers for Disease Control and Prevention (CDC) data from 2018. Recently, the United States recognized its opioid crisis as a national epidemic. Healing this crisis begins with understanding what propels the opioid addict. The CDC estimates a "total economic burden" of 78.5 billion dollars a year. A portion of this "burden" falls into the incompetent hands of the United States' Criminal Justice System.

Much of this epidemic, however, remains something the average person fails to understand.

When friends and family turned their backs and failed to comprehend my struggle with addiction, I relied on "man's best friend" for salvation. Karma, a boxer I rescued while in the heart of addiction, became my reason to exist. She served as the hero of my life.

While the journey to recovery was difficult for both of us, it was her unconditional love that pulled me through. If I have learned anything about recovery, it is that no one ever recovers alone.

Along with the misunderstandings of addiction, there is also a lack of education regarding policing and racism. As a recovering addict and a former member of the police, I am in a unique position to expand upon these issues and bridge the gap of how they are interrelated. While the US has seen unprecedented protests against systemic racism in 2020, it often places the blame on the police, who willingly serve as gatekeepers for the greater Criminal Justice System.

Instead of focusing on the actions and responses the police take while they are in the field, the US needs to refocus on the training police receive in the academy. Through paramilitary training, which includes teaching potential officers to respond to verbal disobedience with physical violence, the police are perpetuating a culture of abuse.

This culture preys on the less fortunate by over-policing and consistently responding with the "next level of force." I have witnessed racism and police brutality, and in each example the deplorable acts went virtually unpunished because of the "thin blue line."

After earning the nickname "Hug-a-Thug" early on while working for a Wisconsin based police department, I quickly realized that the field training program in place would never allow me to develop into the officer I desired to be.

Instead, I was forced to comply to methodology involving the unfair targeting of "those that had shit," in order to prove myself worthy of a position within the department. Although I never set out to be a racist officer, being trained by and requiring approval from others who were racist left me morally bankrupt.

I believe my experience matches that of many young police recruits across the nation and can help explain the public outcry for change we desperately need.

That is the basis for this story: my life with Karma, drug addiction, and criminality to support a habit.

In sobriety, I have maintained ownership over my actions. I have also survived recovery from a traumatic brain injury in jail, paid over 13,000 dollars in restitution and served four years on felony probation.

Like me, those that struggle with addiction often become entangled in the criminal justice system. Once ordinary citizens, these individuals deal with forever labels placed upon them by a system incapable of recognizing personal transformation. A mugshot should not define who I am, nor should it define those in recovery that have devoted their lives to living for a greater purpose.

I felt the need to write about my struggles because I had been quiet for too long. Others like me need a voice. I have kept stories of abuse, sexual harassment, police misconduct, and additional atrocities locked inside. These stories have incessantly eaten away at my essence and further deteriorated my mental well-being.

I have attempted suicide and hospitalization was the only way to restore me to a functioning baseline. Instead of keeping these secrets hidden, I hope to create a greater understanding for those suffering from addiction, police abuse or misconduct, and mental illness through my personal experiences.

The path to restoration lies within my ability to deliver the complete story. No longer will I allow for partial truths to pave my future or the future of others. Instead, I serve as the author of my own story.

IT STARTED WITH A PHONE CALL

———

The morning began like so many others: an unwanted intrusion of a cell phone ring. The subsequent chime indicated a new voicemail had been received. Looking at my phone's clock, I saw it was a few minutes after 10 a.m.

A sleepy secondary glance revealed the caller's number was not saved in my phone. This prompted an immediate red flag, and I began to feel anxious. Was it a sergeant from my department calling to order me in for an overtime shift? Was I going to be on my feet all day instead of laying comfortably in bed? Was I going to have to sweat my ass off in full dress uniform while working a special event?

With my fingers crossed, I anxiously accessed my voicemail. Expecting to hear the voice of an overburdened superior, I dreaded the opening statement.

"Hey Travis, this is Jon, we work out at the Princeton Club together sometimes..."

Click! I hung up the phone before listening to the remainder of the message. No sergeant's voice on the other end meant I could attempt to sleep for a few more hours. It was Saturday after all.

A couple hours of broken sleep later, I found myself making a second attempt to start the day. While my mind still transitioned between dreams and cognition, I rumbled down the stairs like an uncoordinated linebacker and into the kitchen in search of something to eat. There I observed a hastily scribbled note which read something to the effect of, "at the barn, took Bonsai with, be home later."

"So, no wife, no dog and a Saturday afternoon free of responsibility," I thought to myself. In this moment, a typical rookie cop may have turned into a college football game, cracked a beer, and relished having a few free hours of time not consumed by orders.

Yet I was not your standard academy fresh hire.

CHAPTER 1

ALLOW ME TO INTRODUCE MYSELF

———

Before I was sworn into the Wisconsin Capitol Police Department, I already had plenty of all-consuming life experiences. Many of my childhood undertakings were carefully crafted facades, meant to protect the integrity of my father, an alcoholic and a high school principal.

On the surface, we were a picturesque white, nuclear family. Underneath, there were secrets my brother and I were forced to keep.

An example of this is when my father would occasionally take us to his high school's football home games. While driving to the game, he would sip 50/50 Diet Coke and Seagram's Seven Crown as he instructed exactly how to act when we encountered certain individuals.

During these lectures he would warn us, "there would be absolute hell to pay" should we fail to obey his orders. After he parked the car, the charade would begin.

My father would greet everyone with a smile followed by a firm handshake. Meanwhile, my brother and I were instructed not to speak, unless spoken to first. In such cases, we were to be polite, yet terse in our answers. In order to keep our replies short, and to avoid the possibility that we would accidentally divulge a family secret, my father taught us to deflect the conversation back towards the person we were talking to. He would coach us to reply to questions with inquires of our own, stating that "people like to talk about themselves."

I would try my absolute best to actively listen and track adult conversations, all while keeping an eye on my younger sibling. If the encounters went well, we were rewarded with a trip to the eccentric science teacher's room to see the ferrets and whatever other creatures were being kept at the time.

Should my brother or I go off script, or say something unbefitting of the "perfect children," the punishment ranged from verbal onslaughts to physical beatings with a belt. The sentence for our "crimes" rarely corresponded to the act itself. Instead, it was based on how much alcohol our father consumed throughout the course of the evening.

Friday nights spent at the high school football games mirrored most of my early adolescent life. Do exactly as you are told, watch out for your little brother, and know there would be extreme ramifications should you deviate off course. While my mother did the best she could to shield us from our father's abusive behavior, her greatest efforts were often foiled by the volatile nature of an alcoholic, whose best coping method was to continue drinking.

As my father continually altered his state of consciousness, his overall temperament became as fluid as the liquid concoctions he consumed.

On one particularly awful evening of terror, my father stumbled into our bedroom unprovoked. As I was pretending to sleep, he slammed me against the headboard and began striking me in the chest. After a few blows, I urinated myself in fear. I had absolutely no idea what I had done to deserve such a beating. Then just as quickly as the attack began, my father stopped hitting me and departed from the room. He never explained these actions.

The next morning, my mother decided to speak with the Police Liaison Officer (PLO) at the junior high school where she taught. By mid-day, I was called into the office of my elementary school, where I was greeted by the PLO, the principal, and my mother.

After tearfully reliving the events from the prior evening, the police officer confidently explained to me that "steps would be taken to ensure this never happened again."

My spirits were lifted to unprecedented heights, as I clung to the officer's statement. I placed my complete faith in the gathered authority figures, and it appeared I had finally found protection beyond my mother's shield.

Images of my favorite wrestler, the immortal Hulk Hogan masquerading as a police officer, filled my mind. I envisioned my father on the receiving end of Hogan's infamous giant boot, followed by a thunderous leg drop. The lethal finishing combination used to rout countless wrestling heels would undoubtedly be enough to take down my antagonist. Violence used to combat violence was the greatest solution my developing brain could concoct.

Following the deserved Hogan smack down, our lives would subsequently improve. No longer would I have to pretend to be asleep early, in hopes my dad would pass over me after a day of drinking. We wouldn't have to spend our weekends making impromptu trips to our grandparent's house just to "be safe." Perhaps my younger brother would even feel comfortable enough to sleep in his own bedroom. Disappointingly, the "Hulkster" never showed up, the incident was swept under the rug, and the cycle of abuse continued into my teenage years.

Like numerous other depressed teens subjected to violence and maltreatment at home, I eventually rebelled. The mutiny began when I got my driver's license and found freedom the instant I was offered keys to my first car. Shortly after my sixteenth birthday, my parents bought me a late '90s model Toyota Paseo to commute to and from school. The economical car was far from a head turner, but it granted freedom to a larger world — a world beyond the microcosm of a broken home. My car's limits were measured by a fuel gauge and whatever money I had.

After a three-month honeymoon phase, during which friends and I modified the most accessible operating systems (audio and air intake), the Paseo was deemed ready for a maiden cross-country voyage. The destination: Buffalo, NY. Fueling up on wings and visiting female friends was only part of the reason we collectively chose Buffalo. Ultimately, our goal was to see the giant ball drop in the Times Square New Year's Eve celebration and Buffalo served as an ideal hub.

Originally, three of us planned to make the eleven hour, seven-hundred-mile journey together over winter break. Unfortunately, my friend Dave, who was still facing trouble at home stemming from a homecoming curfew violation, bailed roughly a week before the trip. Josh, my best friend since kindergarten and ideal road trip companion, remained a go until the morning of departure when my escape was detected.

My family had two large dogs at the time, who woke up with the sound of the basement door being opened. They immediately barked, alerting my parents that someone was coming or going.

Despite being as stealthy as humanly possible, I was moments away from being caught. Without delay and with my heart racing, I slipped into my car and smashed the garage door opener button. Quickly, I put my car into reverse and barely snuck underneath the ascending door.

With my father's Toyota Celica GT chasing behind me and likely closing quickly, I made the bold decision not to stop and pick up Josh. I also opted not to answer the prepaid cell phone I picked up for the journey. Instead, the note I left in my bedroom detailing where I was going would have to serve as an explanation for my actions.

The now solo voyage was going comparatively well, until I encountered snow outside of Chicago. I had planned for snow, just not the 2000 December nor'easter. The significant winter storm began as an Alberta clipper, traveled southeast, and proceeded to dump snow across the Ohio Valley.

Portions of New York State, including Buffalo, were buried under two feet of powder over the course of the weekend.

Twenty years later, I still recall the white-knuckle grip I kept on the steering wheel, as I desperately tried to keep the fourteen-inch tires aligned with the tracks formed by larger vehicles. With emergency vehicle only travel announcements breaking through on local radio broadcasts, my anxiety rose to unprecedented heights.

Completely exhausted and beyond taxed from driving straight through treacherous winter conditions for the better half of a day, I found lodging on the outskirts of Buffalo. Prior to crashing out for the night, I reluctantly called home to report I had arrived safely and announce my intention to stay the weekend.

My mother imprudently beseeched me to "come home" immediately, while my father coldly asked about the condition of the car and if I had enough money for the return trip. During the short conversation, neither asked the significant question of why?

I spent the remainder of a restless evening, along with an overwhelming portion of the twelve-hour commute home, asking myself that very question. Why?

At the time, the answer seemed relatively simple. I drove to Buffalo to escape the continual distress of spending another winter break at home with an abusive alcoholic. There was also Briton. My long-distance love interest had her own unique backstory from which spawned emotional maturity and overall empathy for my situation. Briton's family home in Buffalo, just like my grandparents' home, was a provisional shelter from a bigger storm.

It was an overly simplified reason, for otherwise irrational behavior. Plus, "traveling to Buffalo to see a girl" was a narrative I could explain to my classmates without compromising my family's fragile secret. The nuclear image would be upheld, and my transgressions eventually forgiven.

Little did I know, this adventure would mark the first recognizable manic episode in a sequence of overlooked bipolar tendencies that would shape the next two decades of my life.

CHAPTER 2

SINS OF OUR FATHERS

At some point in our lives, we all end up paying for the sins of our father(s).

In my family's case, the unanticipated debt came in the fall of 2001. I was a day away from celebrating my eighteenth birthday and two weeks into my senior year. Soccer season was underway, which meant balancing the demands of athletics with a college-centric academic load. I was taking it all in stride, until the local police showed up at our doorstep.

My initial inclination was that the two officers had come to see me. Less than a month prior, I hosted an underage drinking party while my parents were on a trip to Florida. To my knowledge, the party flew under the radar. Now, I feared that my school's administration had received word of the revelry and I was about to face a police inquisition. As I strained to think of an exonerating story, I saw my father removed from the rear seat of the squad car.

He didn't say a word as he brushed past me into the house. Instead, I was left standing there dumbfounded. I could only speculate on what misconduct had just occurred. That evening, I laid sleeplessly in bed, contemplating what could have happened and the trouble my father might be facing.

The local newspaper article ran the next day with the headline: "Lomira principal faces court after shoplifting incident." The write-up described how my father attempted to "conceal a bottle of vodka in the front of his pants." The article went on to say he also tried to steal two canisters of film and a package of toothpicks. According to the police report, the total value of items stolen was $25. Now the entire community knew, and my family had to deal with the fallout.

My father responded to the allegations by stating, "I have a problem with alcohol and need help." He was immediately placed on paid administrative leave while the incident was investigated further by the school district. The community paper continued to cover the story, detailing his resignation in late October, as well as the salary and benefits he would receive through the end of March.

According to the school district's attorney, the compensatory salary received by my father would "fund the help he needed on a personal level." After that, no additional severance package would be offered.

On November 16, 2001, my father pleaded no contest to the shoplifting charge and was ordered to pay a fine of $150.50. While the fine was nominal, the damage to my father's reputation had irreparable consequences.

The public perception our family spent years cultivating was instantaneously eradicated. A plethora of teaching accolades, accompanied by a master's degree in Education Administration, became scrap paper. The lion's head ring, an anniversary gift from my mother and representation of the school's mascot, was good as melt.

My father's identity was based completely around his role as a principal. Everything he did was centered upon his title, and the social standing associated with it. Who was my father without this title? He spent his entire life building toward one role and now it was gone. What was he supposed to do? Over the months that followed, the savings account dwindled, and bills began to pile up. My mother did the best she could, but it was an impossible situation. With only one parent working in public education, it was hard for us to make ends meet. Job prospects for an alcoholic ex-principal were also extremely hard to come by. Regardless of the dire situation, my mother refused to give up. She immediately sought out treatment options, explored alternative career opportunities, and even landed my father a position with a reputable financial planning firm, on the condition he remained sober and learned the material.

While my mother worked to ensure the bills were paid, my father was supposed to be learning a new craft and connecting with a sponsor. Alternatively, he spent his days dejected and isolated in the basement office.

Every time my brother or I would have to venture downstairs to use the computer, we would see him staring blankly at the screen. Little digital fish swimming back and forth indicated he had not accomplished much, if anything at all, during hours of seclusion. I naively maintained hope he was preparing himself for a miraculous comeback, and then the bottles started appearing.

We found bottles hidden everywhere!

Throughout the basement, in the garage, under the seat of his car, resting above drop tiles in the ceiling. We discovered bottles wherever a fifth to a liter sized bottle could fit. When my mother confronted him about our findings, he would get defensive and immediately lash out.

Profanity laden personal attacks, coupled with the occasional projectile, seemed to be his weapons of choice. My brother, Kyle, avoided these assaults by retreating to the confines of his bedroom or escaping on his bicycle. Having had enough of the repeated abuse, my mother filed the paperwork to legally separate. Still, we saw no changes. Distraught and at her wit's end, my mother kicked my father out of our lives in the spring of 2002. The subsequent summer brought additional turmoil into our already tumultuous lives.

On July 15, 2002, my mother filed for divorce. Around the same time, we prepared to put the house on the market. Although I was not fully cognizant of how dire the economic situation had become, intermittent phone calls to grandparents pleading for financial aid were becoming more frequent. While most of my friends were preparing to leave for college, I was working full time for a local landscape company to help cover expenses. As the financial noose continued to tighten, I nearly abandoned the idea of attending college completely, but my mother insisted "things would be alright." With reluctance, I applied for and was accepted to UW-Fond du Lac.

The house eventually sold in early November 2002. With money from the sale, my mother was able to secure a down payment on a smaller house across town. Occasionally she would talk to my father on the phone, but overall, we heard little from him. He returned to his hometown of Menasha, Wisconsin and was working as a sales consultant for a flooring company.

As 2002 changed over into 2003, our lives encountered a fleeting period of stability.

Despite receiving poor academic marks my first semester at UW-Fond du Lac, I passed all my courses. My mother and brother also showed signs of growth, as each found avenues to address their individual areas of damage. My mother focused on her artwork and began creating pieces to display around our new home. My brother turned to soccer and excelled as both goalkeeper and defender.

Like surfers conquering a break, each of us aimed to "ride the wave" for as long as possible. I was the first to fall in the autumn of 2003.

CHAPTER 3

CODE OF ADDICTION

After spending the better half of the summer mastering the nuances of a belt-driven Kawasaki 440 LTD, I was ready for a larger motorcycle. Title in hand, I set out for a nearby dealership to trade-up to a V-twin sport bike produced by Honda, known as the Superhawk.

Acknowledging I was in for a significant increase in power and performance, I tossed on a helmet before riding out. As I exited our neighborhood and turned onto a nearby frontage road, I immediately noticed sporadic patches of leaked oil. Vigilantly, I changed lane positions and continued my journey.

As I made a long sweeping turn, I encountered a massive pool of oil in my lane. When the rear tire of my motorcycle hit the lubricated surface, it immediately kicked out.

I was slammed down on my side with the bike traveling on top of me. Scrapping across the ground at nearly forty mph, I slid over 350 feet on the greased asphalt. Once my world stopped rotating, I struggled to free my leg and foot from under the wreckage.

Fueled by adrenaline, I freed myself from an entanglement of motorcycle pieces. Next, I picked up the dilapidated motorcycle, walked it over to the shoulder and deposited it into the gravel. A motorist who witnessed the accident offered to assist me. As I looked back into her face, I pictured a likeness to Munch's *The Scream*. The conglomerate of debris and blood covering my right arm nearly sent the poor woman into hysterics. Before I could console her, EMTs arrived and handled my transport to a local hospital.

I was treated for severe road rash, a concussion, a fractured foot, and a high ankle sprain. Our family physician said, "if it weren't for that brain bucket, I would be having a much different conversation with your mother... about donating your organs."

After further evaluation, he stated I would possibly need a skin graft to repair damaged tissue around my elbow. I was prescribed OxyContin for the pain, given a plethora of gauzes and anti-bacterial ointment to treat the abrasions, fitted for a walking boot, and released into the custody of my mother for overnight monitoring.

I had never experienced anything like I did when I took my first pill. Much like alcohol has a numbing effect, Oxy works the same way but is so much more potent. As a prescribed medication, OxyContin is the brand name for oxycodone, a slow-release painkiller designed to treat chronic or prolonged pain for up to 12 hours. Shortly after taking OxyContin for pain, I recall feeling what the band Pink Floyd perfectly depicted as being "comfortably numb."

The "miracle" medication mitigated most of the physical agony that stemmed from my body. As I naturally purged remnants of debris, waste oil, and other foreign bodies embedded in the broken layers of dermis, I recall feeling nothing. Even the larger stones, which left bloody divots deep within my skin, barely drew a reaction. I was numb from head to toe.

As the opioids bound to and blocked specific pain receptors, I was granted some semblance of "normal life" merely days after the accident. What appeared to be a triumphant come back, rapidly disintegrated as my relationship with the drug flourished.

The first major side effect I experienced while taking OxyContin was severe lethargy. I recall hobbling to my undergraduate courses, building a complete sweat in the process, only to get situated and pass out before the lecture began. Despite my best efforts to stay awake, the opioid-based drug made me so tired that I would catch myself nodding off at the worst times. Fellow classmates could compare me to a life-sized bobblehead, as my head continually fell toward my chest.

Even in a waking state, I was unable to focus on the information conveyed by the professor. Instead, my cognition floated somewhere between a dream and reality. Fragments of information would take brief footholds, only to be displaced by new data prior to being encoded in my memory. Essentially, I was not amassing new knowledge while taking OxyContin and subsequently unable to recall said information down the line. This proved troublesome in the realm of college academia.

Even more difficult to conquer than chemically induced narcolepsy was the mood swings I faced on OxyContin. I recollect experiencing waves of emotion virtually devoid of correlation to daily life. One moment, I would be happy and feel as if I were floating. Moments later, I would be depressed and battling the urge to put my head down and sleep.

Just as I struggled with emotional regulation, personal relationships become strained and difficult to manage. I had a friend who couldn't understand what the big deal was when he picked up the wrong brand of beer for a weekend outing. When deciding what movie to go to, my girlfriend was taken back when I launched into a tirade about Jim Carrey and how much I hated his face. Within a couple weeks of taking Oxy, my social life was trending toward extinction. I began to feel secluded and self-isolated even more.

Justifying the self-imposed quarantine through the rationalization that my trauma was terminally unique; I never allotted my peers the opportunity to show empathy. Instead, I pushed those away who were trying to be supportive. Perhaps, it was because I didn't understand my blooming relationship with the drug well enough to explain it to anyone. Consequently, several friends discredited my affliction, and we continued to grow apart.

As the totality of circumstances impeding recovery from the motorcycle accident grew, I opted to withdraw from college for the semester. The objective was to concentrate on healing prior to re-enrolling in coursework over the summer. Unbeknownst to me, the summer of 2004 was about to permanently re-prioritize my life.

CHAPTER 4

UNFORTUNATE SON

Being the firstborn child into any family comes with an indeterminate set of added responsibilities. Prominent theorists have published studies pertaining to the influence that birth order plays in shaping an individual's overall lifestyle. While the findings of these studies have been met with a fair amount of criticism, I believe the following to be collectively true.

The greater amount of dysfunction that occurs within the family unit, the greater the obligation the eldest child feels to take corrective action.

This phenomenon often ensues regardless of the firstling's preparation or capacity to effectively manage the situation at hand. By detailing the events that shaped the hypothesis above, I aim to offer a "mirror" of familiarity for those who stepped into a parentified role too soon.

While rehabilitating from the motorcycle accident, I eventually weaned off Oxycontin onto a "safer" medication, to assist with overall pain management. At first, I hated my primary care physician for swapping out the "miracle medication." The common OTC pain medicine he prescribed to replace the opioid functioned as a mere placebo.

Not only did I begin to feel pain again, but intense feelings of crippling anxiety came crashing down upon me at inopportune times. Throughout the day, I felt unmanageable stress that was disproportionate to the day's events. Something as simple as a trip to the grocery store could invoke fear and apprehension. My inability to set worry aside, drove me into a constant state of restlessness.

After nightfall, countless hours of darkness crawled by, as I laid awake plagued by recurring thoughts. Fractured friendships drove me further into seclusion, and my mood plummeted to the point that I was sad and lonely most of the time. As the persistent negative thoughts went unspoken, they gained influence and began to control my internal narrative. Soon, I couldn't stop thinking of suicide. This mindset overwhelmed me to the point where I no longer saw a future. Before I knew it, I was breaking off commitments and abandoning all of my long-term plans.

Then something happened that put my suicide plans on hold; my father landed in the hospital. We were told he might not have long to live.

At the time my father was admitted into the hospital, we had not spoken for several months. The last time I saw him, he showed up at my mother's new house drunk and started yelling at my brother and me. When he attempted to enter my brother's room, I blocked his way. On some level, I felt like I needed to protect my brother from him.

Previously, such action would have resulted in a physical altercation, but my father conceded without a fight. At the time I attributed the triumph to the additional muscle mass I gained during rehabilitation and weight training.

In retrospect, I realized that my father didn't fight back because he was a broken man.

After hitting rock bottom, alcoholism continued to claim what remained of my father's shattered natural life. Less than two years had passed since my mother filed for divorce and yet it was enough time for his addiction to claim victory. When we arrived at the hospital to visit him, I hardly recognized the shell of the bedridden man before me.

His skin was an unnatural tone of yellow. His legs had swollen to the size of fire hydrants. When he spoke to me, the words were labored and interrupted by a menacing cough. Although I hated him for years of abuse and mistreatment, it was haunting to see him so close to death. Despite the intense inclination to run out of the room, I stayed.

In that moment, I tried to tell my dad that I forgave him. However, like a true principal, he led the conversation.

In a strained voice, he asked that I continue to protect my mother and brother. I assured him I would. After making the promise, I asked if there was anything else he needed. Trying to make light of the situation, he asked if I could help him get up and go to the bathroom, "now that I had muscles." We both chuckled, he began coughing uncontrollably, and a nurse promptly ushered me from the room.

That was the last conversation I had with my father.

On July 12, 2004, Patrick James Sackett died at St. Elizabeth Hospital in Appleton, WI. He was 51 years old. The medical professionals stated he died from complications related to cirrhosis of the liver.

At some point, his kidneys were overtaxed by the copious amounts of alcohol he consumed and ceased to function. As toxins built up within his body, his liver entered a state of failure, ultimately resulting in his premature death. While I may not have highlighted the best parts of my father's life, I believe he would appreciate my authenticity. Having spent years keeping secrets and hiding from the truth, my father's opportunity to be honest surpassed him. Consequently, I carry his burden of truth.

Alcoholism killed my father and corrupted his mind. When left to their own devices, many alcoholics suffer similar fates. As they slowly die internally, the external damage caused by their actions is devastating to those who love them. My father died disconnected from our family because he continued drinking and refused to seek help. Sobriety could have saved him; instead, he found solace at the bottom of another bottle.

Living sober will always trump not living at all. I wish my father would have viewed his life with a similar perspective.

CHAPTER 5

PERSONAL REPRESENTATIVE

———

My father died without a will. Since he had not named an executor, I was appointed by the probate court to administer the estate.

I was completely overwhelmed by the process of managing an estate. I was just about to turn 21 and the fall semester was about to begin. I didn't know the first thing about the probate process! Thankfully, my mother hired an attorney to assist me.

The greatest impediment to closing the estate was rectifying medical claims or bills accrued while my father was hospitalized.

Working diligently with the estate attorney, I found purpose. The challenges presented to a full-time undergraduate balancing an appointed personal representative role kept my mind engaged. I immersed myself in course work and estate claims, leaving little free time to focus on anything else. This included grieving.

Instead, patience, an abstract concept to many college students, became my modus operandi. Every assignment, medical claim, and court correspondence was met with intense diligence. I refused to let my family suffer additional losses simply because I didn't have my shit together. Fear of failure drove me toward meticulousness. Work became my salvation.

My 21st birthday came and went without celebration or ritual rite of passage. Instead of accepting invitations to parties and allowing alcohol to numb my pain, I opted for a year of self-imposed sobriety. It was my belief that if I could "win the battle" against alcohol, then my father would have not died in vain.

I linked my sobriety to my departed father's legacy. This pairing drove me even closer to perfectionism. For that year, I remained hyper-focused on school and settling the estate; barely even thinking of booze.

It was revitalizing to experience such a dramatic turn of events. The seasons changed without me noticing, and I continued to improve my scholastic standing. My college GPA, which was a dismal 1.7 following the aftermath of the motorcycle accident, rocketed to over 3.0.

With the drastic increase in my GPA, the possibility of transferring to a 4-year program also became a reality. Doors that had seemingly closed, were now opening. On the surface, one could argue that I was "adjusting well" and "coping with the loss."

In truth, I selected action over grief. Ultimately, I refused to mourn while my family needed a rock. Instead, I systematically collected the pieces of my father's broken life and got to work. Once I understood what my father left unfinished, I was able to pick up where he left off. It was difficult managing the truncated tasks, but a sense of accomplishment followed every time I crossed an item from the list. With the estate to-do list shrinking, I switched focus toward my future.

As I began mulling over options for continued college education, the estate neared completion of the probate process. Over twenty-five thousand dollars in medical bills were disbursed and any outstanding child support claims were rectified.

Nearly one year later, on August 22, 2005, the estate was closed, and the case was settled. Having successfully completed the probate process would have left many feeling proud or accomplished. I recall feeling empty.

Closing the estate implied that my father was gone forever. Furthermore, it allotted space and time for actual mourning. Subsequently, I had no idea how to mourn a father that I spent most of my existence fearing.

Alternatively, I reconnected with my childhood best friend Josh. Together, we decided to become roommates and move onto a college campus roughly forty-five minutes from home. The distance allowed for the space to grow independently, with the ability to return home within an hour should something arise.

As summer ended, I found myself transitioning once again. No longer was I responsible for probate processes or rectifying medical claims. Instead, I was finally free to act my age. Only issue was, I had no idea what that looked like.

It wasn't until move-in day that I began to understand my new roll. As we unloaded our cars, Josh and I both cracked a beer. It was my first in over a year and instantly tasted like freedom. It also represented the first of many infractions I would commit while living in the dry, co-ed dorm.

Despite the rules set forth by the college, Josh and I were determined to live the complete college experience. Together, we were about to carve out a legacy at the "college in the cornfield."

CHAPTER 6

COLLEGE IN
A CORNFIELD

When Lakeland College's admission team authorized two Junior transfer students to join the ranks of the undergraduates on its rural campus, they drastically underestimated the impact one dyad could have on an isolated population.

Josh, who you may recall as the friend who was left behind during the chaos as I departed for Buffalo, served as my unequivocal partner in crime. Companions since kindergarten, Josh and I maintained a bond like brotherhood.

As a stand-in brother, Josh and I shared many life "firsts."

It was with Josh in high school that I first got drunk with over a bottle of blue raspberry UV Vodka. Josh was the one who taught me how to ride a motorcycle, rebuild a carburetor, and to take pride in the process of creating something outside of yourself. Throughout the years leading up to our departure for college, Josh ushered in a plethora of new activities and introduced me to a crew of diverse individuals. Without Josh, my social life would have been relatively mundane.

Above all, Josh served as my life liaison. His presence ensured that no matter how horrendous home was, I would always have a person or outlet to escape some of the pain. Josh's family home served as my sanctuary, much like my grandparent's home when I was younger. Josh's parents were also consistently chill, and their relaxed vibe always served to calm my anxiety.

After fifteen years of shared adventures, with a brief hiatus after my father died, time and circumstance assigned us a new title. We were officially roommates.

As roommates, our primary goal at our new school was to live the "college experience." We decided to measure this intangible with two metrics.

The first, a tally counter, which was mounted between our desks and utilized to track every alcoholic beverage we consumed throughout the semester. Essentially, a drinking scoreboard with very strict rules, which included how every drink had to be verified prior to being added to the running total.

This practice typically transpired as we debriefed after a night out. Sometimes, we would make tally marks on our arms to track the number of beverages we consumed. Other times, we conducted morning counts of the empties we accumulated after an "average" evening drinking in our dorm room. Either way, we documented the copious amounts of alcohol we consumed to the best of our ability.

The second tool we utilized to measure our college success was the same standardized measurement our professors were using to track our academic achievement, our grades.

Despite the goal to live the ultimate college experience, we both realized the weight that maintaining stellar GPAs carried. Transferring in as Juniors, each of us could recite stories of high school classmates going off to college, partying too hard and being placed on academic probation within a semester. Typically, these individuals would falter again the next semester and their college experience would conclude less than a year from its inception. Instead of allowing one another to slip academically, we competed to see who could post the highest score or pull a better grade. Pushing one another scholastically, allowed us to party passionately with diminished consequences. Furthermore, we shared many of the same criminal justice classes. Our projects, papers, and tests typically coincided with one another, so we often had the same evenings dedicated to our coursework.

As we toiled through academia, we both consumed the exclusive moments that could only be captured in the college microcosm. These personal experiences produced long-term memories that I will carry with me for the duration of my life. For example, I'll never forget streaking across the open field that separated the dorms simply to fulfill a coed's dare. Ultimately, the more gratifying Josh and I were able to make the process of higher education, the more memorable the people who were a part of the process became.

Documenting our nights of debauchery could easily fill the remaining pages of this manuscript. However, I aim to transcribe a tale deeper than the conquests of two college adolescents. Instead, the following paragraphs provide a summary of what the college experience taught me.

Grasping onto the traditional narrative regarding colleges' goal to "prepare an individual to engage in purposefully work" is dated and deeply misguided. Alternatively, it is critical to comprehend the metrics on which one is being evaluated.

Ultimately, our social system has built in standards or expectations for our individual performance at select milestones throughout our existence. While many college graduates will argue the importance of deriving a sense of purpose from their daily work, few can proudly state their work after college provides gratifying motivation.

Instead, it is imperative that each individual find their own pleasure in the process.

I will always remember the times I shared with Josh and others at Lakeland College. Despite drinking too much and learning just enough, I left college with a better understanding of who I was. I still had no idea of what I would become, but at least I gained life experience beyond the expectations of others.

I was finally paving my own path, but little did I know, the path would lead directly back home.

CHAPTER 7

CORNFIELDS TO CORPORATE GYMS

After graduating from Lakeland College in the fall of 2007, I was uncertain as to how I wanted to pursue a career. I achieved a Bachelor of Arts in Criminal Justice and placed check marks in many of the boxes potential employers expressed interest.

At Lakeland, I acted as Vice President of the school's chapter of the American Criminal Justice Association, as well as Student's Against Excessive Drinking (SAED). As VP of SAED, I frequently provided others advice on how to drink responsibly, despite having consumption issues of my own. Although I felt like a hypocrite, I knew the role would look good on future resumes and omit me from having to justify how much I once drank to potential employers. After all, who would assume the VP of SAED would have an alcohol issue?

Aside from the two VP roles, I also served as a Campus Ambassador for the College, while providing site tours for prospective students. I even dressed as the school's mascot, a giant blue fish named Musko, and attended local high school football games to "hype the crowd" while promoting the college.

On paper, I was the poster child for endorsing the institution while adding value to existing student organizations. After leaving Lakeland College, however, I struggled to find my place in the working world.

As a Criminal Justice major, the primary vocational options were limited to the fields of private security, policing, and corrections. I was leaning toward policing because I wanted to protect people, especially those in abusive situations. Pursuing a career in policing, however, would also require an additional 520-hour police academy. Furthermore, I would have to self-sponsor for the academy, which called for additional funds that I frankly did not have.

Realizing the need to obtain gainful employment, I attended the pre-sale campaign of a corporate owned franchise gym that was opening in my hometown.

Initially, I was seeking a position as a personal trainer. Instead, I was sold on the "opportunity" to create a gym member base from scratch, while acting as the General Manager.

By accepting the GM position, I was promised a small percentage of membership dues from each new member I signed up, on top of a low hourly wage. Additionally, if the new member was to pay in full, or PIF, I would be compensated more for the sale compared to a membership that was billed monthly.

As opposed to filling the next few pages with how I grew the member base from zero to over six hundred in less than seven months, I'm opting to expose the "trade secrets" that helped me do so.

When touring any gym as a consumer, one must remember that at some point they are going to try to sell you their service. This may sound simple; however, potential members are frequently baited into the gym with limited-time promotional flyers or through a lead box contest "win."

For example, I was instructed by ownership to place lead boxes throughout the community. These boxes offered individuals a chance at winning a free yearly membership or similar prize. For the entry to be valid, each person would provide their name along with contact information.

Every week I would collect the lead boxes, call each completed entry form, and say the following in the most excited/ upbeat voice possible; "Hey, this is Travis over at 24/7 Fitness. I'm calling to let you know that you won a free trial membership with us. What is the best time for you to stop by and pick it up?"

Next, I would provide one of two options for pickup. Ideally the winner would be scheduled for the same day, worst case a day or two in the future. Once a time was agreed upon, the individual was immediately slated for a facility tour.

Upon arrival, each prospective member was acknowledged and welcomed within thirty seconds of walking through the door. Next, they were instantly asked to complete a new member profile.

The profile posed as a harmless introductory questionnaire; however, it was covertly geared toward identifying potential "objections" that one may face during the sales process. Essentially, each question asked corresponded to a potential objection a future member may offer.

For example, the question of "What has held you back from joining a gym in the past?" exposes the justifications the prospective member may offer when declining to join the gym.

Subsequently, the more objections that are faced and closed during the tour, the easier it becomes to sell the prospective member during the sales presentation. The seemingly harmless answers provided on the new member profile eliminate opportunities for a prospect to provide modest objections or a straightforward "no."

After completing the rapport building tour, it's on to the sales presentation.

The sales presentation is essentially a series of tie-downs, or statements which allow the salesperson to control the conversation. During my sales presentation, I utilized a binder with three pieces of material.

The first was a diagram explaining muscle mass and metabolism. Essentially, I explained why some people can "eat whatever they want and not gain weight." Next came a success or crusade story from an existing member regarding his/her triumphant weight loss journey. This material was commonly coupled with an action/training plan, meant to show the prospective member their goal was obtainable, had been achieved by others, and could be broken down into manageable steps.

After establishing how often a member will attend the gym per week, the final thing one must determine is a financially comfortable budget. To do so, I introduced a tiered membership pricing breakdown with an incentive to purchase that day.

For example, if you sign up today, "I can waive the new member fee along with giving you the first month on us." Essentially, this is the final sales pitch where the deal is closed with an offer "too sweet to pass up."

Sometimes an individual would hit me with an objection during this phase, to which I would use what we had already talked about to counter their argument. Previous answers became ammunition for shooting down last-minute objections to purchasing a membership.

Hardly ever would I allow an individual to escape the office without being subjected to a hard close had they continued to offer "excuses." Most of the time, individuals feel victim to the sales process and were christened new members before realizing they had been sold.

So, why take the time to expose a common, yet seedy industry sales tactic?

Transparency... transparency for what is yet to come.

Working for 24/7 Fitness was the first time I felt uncomfortable performing my job. As opposed to speaking out against the process, I let ownership create dual justifications for my behavior.

The first rationale was that "nearly everyone could benefit more from working out" and thus would benefit from becoming a gym member. I was sold on this credo during the job interview and allowed it to root into my sales rhetoric without protest.

Secondly, I needed the commission from each sale to rectify the otherwise poor base pay I was receiving. Without prioritizing new member sales, I was not able to take home enough pay to support my regular bills.

At the end of the day, sales drove my paycheck. My paycheck dictated how I lived on a biweekly basis. Therefore, I justified "selling fitness" to individuals that would likely be better served by a dietitian or counselor.

To all of you reading this who have struggled with a weight loss journey, I make my first apology. I apologize for lengthening your journey, while I profited in the short-term. I was wrong to work for an industry that continues to reap revenue driven by battles with bullies, insecurity, and even self-loathing.

My wish today is that we all find comfort in what we have become.

CHAPTER 8

520 HOURS OF BASIC TRAINING

—

Seven months after I began working for 24/7 Fitness, I was fired.

It was the first time I had been fired from a job and the reason behind my termination had nothing to do with performance. Instead, I was dismissed because I applied for a position through the Department of Corrections. When a recruiter contacted the owner for a job reference, I was visited the same afternoon and told, "this gym needs an individual committed to its long-term success; you are no longer suited for the manager position."

Although being fired was less than ideal, it allowed me to apply for unemployment while pursuing other career aspirations.

At the time, I knew the Department of Corrections hiring process would take a minimum of three, most likely six months. This afforded me time to further research self-sponsoring, or paying my own way, for a law enforcement academy. Even though I found a ton of recruit academies throughout the State of Wisconsin, there just weren't any spots available. Most of these spots were already taken by department sponsored cadets. Without experience, I didn't stand a chance. How could I compete with individuals that were already hired into their position before they had even started their training? In my experience, these individuals also received admittance preference over those who self-sponsored. This resulted in the unclaimed spots being limited and extremely competitive.

When I applied for the Fox Valley Technical College (FVTC) Law Enforcement 520 Academy in 2008, the program was touted as being specifically designed for applicants with a minimum of sixty accredited college-level credits. Since I had already obtained a Bachelor of Arts in Criminal Justice, I figured I had a decent chance of acceptance.

Furthermore, this specific academy was close enough to home that I could make the daily commute without having to find housing. This made FVTC Academy an affordable option compared with similar programs that would require relocation. After two interviews, I was placed on a short list of self-sponsored recruits and was eventually accepted into the Fall Academy.

Many police recruits, including myself, entered the academy as optimists. We believed our future endeavors held the key to transforming individual lives for the better. Unlike the liberal arts college in the cornfield, however, at the police academy "free thinking" was not encouraged.

My classmates and I were immediately assigned seats, stripped of our uniqueness, and provided with uniforms to wear daily. The uniforms consisted of an issued t-shirt, black Battle Dress Uniform (BDU) pants, and "brilliantly shined patrol boots" that were only to be worn while attending classes. On the first day of the academy, I was forced to do push-ups when one of my boots exhibited a small toe scuff. For the first time, I realized I had joined a paramilitary organization. This sort of desensitized training turns idealists into cynics.

As Georgetown law professor Rosa Brooks exclaimed in an article to *The Atlantic,* many police academies deem "brilliantly shined boots are the hallmark to the police uniforms; they indicate devotion to duty and attention to the smallest detail," (Brooks, 2020). However, Brooks proceeded to challenge this rational, later stating:

"When recruits are ordered to do push-ups to the point of exhaustion because their boots aren't properly polished, they may learn the value of attention to detail—but they may also conclude that the infliction of pain is an appropriate response to even the most trivial infractions," (Brooks, 2020).

Although, I felt the academy training placed far too much emphasis on "wrong lessons" of paramilitary teaching, I dared not speak out for fear of punishment. I was afraid to challenge the chain of command because the rigid structure did not allow a soldier to question a superior's order. Instead, we acted as a flock of suppressed sheep, herded by overtly aggressive cattle dogs. While some instructors plainly conveyed orders, others opted to bark them with voracity.

I was yelled at more frequently during my time at FVTC police academy than when I was living with a verbally abusive alcoholic father.

In fact, many of the instructors reminded me of my father regarding how they carried themselves and demanded respect without reciprocation. Extrapolate further, and one begins to see the connection between paramilitary police training and the continued law enforcement exploitations plaguing our nation.

If we groom police recruits through belittlement and stoicism, are we not subconsciously endorsing the same tactics to be deployed in the field?

During a defense and arrest tactics (DAAT) course, I fractured two ribs while holding the striking pad for a partner. At the time of the incident, we were practicing knee strikes to the body of a standing opponent. My partner, who resembled an undersized NFL linebacker, connected squarely with the pad on a first strike, but delivered a second strike prior to my recovery. His softball sized knee wrapped around the edge of the pad and caught me below the elbow, landing directly in my rib cage.

Although he delivered the strike perfectly as a trained technique, direct damage to my ribs and surrounding cartilage was the outcome. Had I been a smaller individual, such a blow would have been utterly devastating. Byway of the training standards at the time, this was considered a control technique, or means of controlling someone who is not complying to verbal commands.

Fundamentally, the academy was teaching that the infliction of pain is an appropriate and trained response to repeated verbal noncompliance.

As we examine the physical abuses administered by domestic law-enforcement throughout our nation, it is necessary to question the training practices propelling the violence.

Throughout the United States, we continue to teach officers that the appropriate response to force is levying the next higher level of force against your combatant. In doing so, we are condoning the killing of roughly 1,000 Americans per year, "a per capita rate of violence unparalleled in other democratic countries", according to law professor Rosa Brooks. (Brooks, 2020).

Pigmentation, the natural coloring of one's dermis, further indicates the probability of violence occurring. "Police violence is a leading cause of death for young men, and young men of color face exceptionally high risk of being killed by police," (Edwards, 2019). Like southern slave patrols once operated, today's police are far too fast to murder a dark skinned individual out of unfounded fear.

Fear that has been instilled over generations of ignorance coupled with systemic racism survives today through an us versus them mentality.

If we want today's police force to be influential, we must stop defeating police recruits in the preliminary stages of training., We should cultivate an environment that praises empathy and aims at enhancing emotional intelligence, instead of criticizing cadets for free thinking.

If the public's expectation for officers is to demonstrate discretion, should we not focus on providing ample training designed to enhance one's decision-making ability?

As an alternative to spending the entirety of the academy building like-minded individuals, it would behoove administrators to prioritize ample community interaction. After all, what separates members of the military from those on the police force? Surely, they are set up to provide different types of enforcement. Therefore, dispersing cadets into society to encounter economic disparity, mental instability, and homelessness could serve as early opportunities to learn how to effectively converse with populations traditional police commonly fail.

Advancing understanding and acceptance amongst the future gatekeepers of the criminal justice system is a start to building the empathetic guardians the United States needs.

CHAPTER 9

$19.95 AN HOUR TO PROTECT THE GOVERNOR

———

Prior to graduating from the Fox Valley Technical College Law Enforcement 520 Academy, I applied for an opening with the Wisconsin State Capitol Police Department. The Division of Capitol Police immediately appealed to me because of the role they serve in safeguarding the governor and their family.

The Capitol Police Dignitary Protection unit is responsible for providing the governor with protection, twenty-four hours a day, seven days a week, at the State Capitol Building or the Executive Residence. In addition to general protective services, the Dignitary unit also secures numerous state-sponsored special events.

The further I investigated the job, the more I realized I was interested in a long-term position. I did everything in my power to elevate my standing on the prospective employer's candidate list. I wanted nothing more than to offer safety and protection to the governor that I was not afforded as a child. I believed that keeping Wisconsin's highest ranking official safe would help ensure the unadulterated operation of the state executive branch.

Given the uniqueness of the role, I felt that working for the Capitol Police could provide workplace gratification that traditional police departments could not rival. After all, how often does one get to protect a high-ranking official? One can only imagine how elated I was when I was invited to participate in the interview process.

As I recall, the entire hiring process took approximately six months. It was comprised of a preliminary application, an initial interview, a lengthy department application, an extensive background investigation including a home visit, a panel interview, and finally psychological and physical testing. The process itself was a practice in patience.

Weeks would pass between objectives without any feedback being provided. Even a decade later, I still remember anxiously awaiting the arrival of the mail each day, only to feel dejected when nothing came. Finally, after months of fulfilling application objectives, I was offered a position with the Wisconsin State Capitol Police Department.

In March 2009, I was sworn into service by Chief Charles A. Tubbs. Immediately following the short ceremony at the state capitol building, I was introduced to members of the Patrol Operations section, along with the Support Services section, who provided communications and dispatch services for the entire department. It all felt rather anticlimactic, compared to months of waiting and jumping through hoops.

At that time, I also convened with the first of three Field Training Officers (FTO), a bear of a man that we will refer to as FTO Matt. The biggest takeaway from my initial meeting with FTO Matt was he seemed rigid and unyielding in his approach. Over the next several weeks, however, I learned that FTO Matt had greater character depth than his gruff exterior revealed.

Throughout his career, FTO Matt cultivated relationships with individuals ranging from working politicians to local homeless. While each population carried a different set of needs, Matt treated everyone with dignity and respect.

During our time training together, Matt shared a story about a time when he was forced to "eat from food donation boxes" to survive. From that day forward, I understood why Matt was able to seamlessly relate to individuals stemming from such diverse backgrounds.

Despite his ability to convey information to diverse populations, FTO Matt struggled as a teacher. Some of the most basic core competencies required of a patrol officer were all but lost under Matt's tutelage. For example, Matt showed me how to effectively work with the capitol's homeless population, even though he couldn't quote a majority of the most commonly used state statutes. Matt's ability to teach me the streets of Madison was also suspect at best.

Coming from a small city with a population under forty thousand people, I wrestled with learning the streets of Madison. Having grown up where directions were based around the location of the county pool or the corner Dairy Queen, it was nearly impossible for me to navigate by street names. I just didn't get it. I found myself getting lost driving across town, let alone going to specific places. Prior to smart phones, I relied heavily on printed MapQuest directions to find where I was going. Even more troublesome were the subsequent locations of the state-owned buildings, which were scattered haphazardly throughout the city.

Despite my best efforts, I struggled to memorize the complex array of one-way streets stemming from the capitol building and failed to grasp how some streets mysteriously changed names as one traveled off the central isthmus. Facing pressure from the department, I opted to spend my days off commuting over an hour to Madison, merely to drive the streets I would be patrolling during the upcoming week. Completely exasperated after hours of driving, I cried most of the return trips home.

Overall, my anxiety grew under the guidance of FTO Matt because I wasn't grasping some of the basics, such as city street layout. I was so fearful that I wouldn't effectively learn the streets that I wanted to quit and give up my dream job. It was not until a galvanizing event, which resulted in the evacuation of the state capitol, that my confidence began to rebuild.

On April 6, 2009, a plane stolen from Canada was reported to be flying erratically and the pilot was not communicating. The plane was approximately 20 minutes away from the capitol building and continued to ignore commands from escorting F-16 fighter jets.

FTO MATT and I were a part of a team of officers and dispatchers that successfully evacuated the state capitol and neighboring justice building. The information our team shared from the event was broadcast on a national level and acclaimed to be the most accurate of all agency submissions.

Although the stolen plane passed by the capitol and was eventually forced to land, I received recognition for job knowledge, quick response, and dealing with difficult people in a time of crisis.

Given the totality of circumstances surrounding the evacuation, I went on to receive an Excellent Service Award on

November 10, 2009. This recognition helped restore some additional confidence I lost during the initial round of field training. After struggling through portions of training with FTO Matt, I was passed on to third shift FTO Dan.

FTO Dan had already served a plethora of years with the Capitol Police and was past the point of burnout when I was assigned to him. He could best be described as R.O.D or retired on duty. Dan shared a wealth of knowledge with me, including the state-owned buildings with the cleanest bathrooms, the best lounges for leisure reading, and which vending machines had the widest variety of late-night snacks. FTO Dan had the work ethic of a teenage stoner.

In all fairness, he also worked part time for another police department, so he frequently came into work exhausted. After all, I was only making $19.95 per hour, so Dan couldn't have been making that much more despite his years of service. Many officers, including Dan, counted on overtime or part-time work to supplement the otherwise relatively low hourly base pay. Seeing officers act like zombies after working extended shifts no longer surprised me, especially once I understood the earnings breakdown.

While working under FTO Dan's tutelage, I also learned to never accept home brew coffee from another officer. One evening, I forgot to pick up an energy drink on the way to work. FTO Dan kindly offered his caffeinated creation, which he described as "having a kick." The bitter dark roast kept me up for nearly twenty-four hours straight.

Although I did not enhance my police skills during FTO Dan's portion of field training, I had ample time to learn the streets and building locations. Overall, FTO Dan's lack of preparation made FTO Matt seem like trainer of the year.

After several complacent weeks with Dan, I had no idea what to expect from my final FTO Eric. FTO Eric was a different breed. He smoked cigarettes like FTO Dan slammed coffee. He also taught me the common police mantra, "shit has shit." This meant that while we were patrolling our second shift, I should constantly be on the lookout for "rusted out cars" or "vehicles displaying damage," or other signs of decay.

Coincidentally, we often found said vehicles in low-income neighborhoods, predominantly inhabited by minority groups.

Whenever we were not performing building checks or completing field training exercises the other two FTOs neglected, FTO Eric and I were pounding traffic. In fact, he even used to say, "let's go play in traffic" after we had performed our other duties, as if controlling people's freedom was simply an act of play.

Initially, I believed FTO Eric was trying to demonstrate the most efficient way to conduct a traffic stop with guaranteed probable cause to stop the vehicle. Today, I realize he was just another racist cop justifying his prejudiced actions through loopholes in the law.

FTO Eric plainly taught me to prey on the less fortunate and then validate the rationale behind the stop with the corresponding state statute. For example, I would stop a vehicle in an over-policed neighborhood for a minor infraction such as broken taillight lens, while constantly fishing for a more sizable violation. This included requesting to search the vehicle, which FTO Eric could articulate as a training opportunity.

Most of the time, my flimsy request to search was denied, as the request itself was never really warranted. I spent weeks learning different tactics to build a routine traffic stop into potential criminal activity as opposed to focusing my efforts on supportive community policing. To make matters worse, my actions were applauded by other second shift officers, further confusing what concocted quality police work. We didn't work on a quota system, nor were our squads equipped with radar, so I never truly understood FTO Eric's motive to pound traffic.

By the time I completed field training, I was utterly perplexed by the objective of patrol work.

Fortunately, I was assigned to the Dignitary Protection Unit, where the primary objective was security. Security, or the state of being free from danger or violence, seemed straightforward. That was the case until I met the Senior Dignitary Protection officer that forever changed the way I view police and the corresponding culture.

CHAPTER 10

PORNOGRAPHY AND VIDEO GAMES

When I was told I would be joining the Dignitary Protection Unit, I expected to be surrounded by some of the finest professionals Wisconsin law enforcement had to offer.

Some of my coworkers matched my expectations. These individuals strived to preserve a standard of excellence, while maintaining the expertise one would expect from an individual protecting Wisconsin's highest-ranking official. Others allowed the clout of the position to adversely influence their discretion and risk the entire unit's integrity.

My initial response to meeting the senior officer, DK7, was instantaneous mistrust. The man, who reminded me of a used car salesperson, touted nearly three decades of law enforcement experience. At this stage in his career, DK7 openly believed his time served acted as a quantifier for his superior and misogynistic behavior.

DK7 was equally brash as he was abrasive.

He often demeaned female members of the Executive Residence's volunteer docents, without provocation. Picture your prototypical grandmother being bullied for no reason other than gender and status of position. Departmental rumor was DK7 once drove for the governor and his wife but was dismissed from the position after a verbal disagreement with Wisconsin's First Lady. Nonetheless, he remained in service and was assigned exclusively to first shift security, 7 a.m. to 3 p.m., at the governor's mansion.

One Tuesday morning, a few months after being assigned to the unit, I was filling in for DK7. I am certain it was a Tuesday because the governor was hosting a cabinet meeting and public tours were slated to be held later that day.

While remotely granting cabinet members access through the mansion's front gates, I mistakenly identified a new model Lincoln sedan with tinted windows and allowed a civilian tourist early unauthorized access. This was a breach of protocol, which dictated I should have verbally confirmed the visitor's commerce prior to opening the gate. Complicating the matter further, the individual that I granted access to was black, whereas most of the governor's cabinet were light skinned. My mistake rightfully caused some upheaval amongst the Executive Residence staff, and I was forced to formally document my error and directly report the blunder to my sergeant.

Taking immediate ownership of the error, coupled with the non-threatening nature of the breach, allowed me to continue working for the Dignitary Protection unit.

However, DK7 felt it was his place to scold me further after hearing rumors of my transgression. He bombarded me with a cascade of insults, including personal attacks about "being a complete fucking meathead" and "that I should go back to running a gym." Furthermore, to "make things simple for me," DK7 stated, "the only n*****s that I should ever allow through the gates are the governor's sons." It is worth noting that the governor had two adopted black male sons.

I should have immediately reported the racist prick, but I was already on thin ice with the department. Furthermore, DK7 built strong rapport with our sergeant throughout the years, meaning I would have to report him directly to a colleague. Instead of trying my luck with the chain of command, I turned my attention toward learning more about DK7 and what drove him to act like such a pompous asshole. Straightaway, I utilized some of the investigative skills I acquired throughout life and living with an alcoholic parent to launch a secret probe into DK7's work habits.

A lead from the executive chef yielded that DK7 typically kept the security door closed, locked, and window shades drawn during his shift. A fellow officer on our unit also alerted me that DK7 was receiving personal phone calls from "females other than his wife" on the officer designated phone line. Immediately, my thoughts concentrated on infidelity, which would help explain his moodiness and cagey actions.

It wasn't until I reported early for an event and accidentally caught a second shift officer with his video gaming system, that I was shown the true evidence of DK7's indiscretions. In an act of exchange for my silence, the embarrassed officer took me into an underutilized portion of the mansion's basement where extra lockers served as storage for the department. There he showed me a plethora of pornography. This included DVDs and magazines belonging to DK7 that were secretly being stored in the basement of the governor's home. Not only was the material titled and geared toward the denigration of women, but it specifically focused on black women.

Like a puzzle with newly found pieces, I now had a more complete picture of DK7's vice.

I allowed a week to pass before taking any action regarding the hidden pornography and my coworker's apparent addiction. During that time, I contemplated what I was taught in the academy regarding officer loyalty, along with respecting the chain of command.

Departmental protocol dictated that I report the infraction to my immediate supervisor, but I was not comfortable with that option given the close relationship DK7 shared with our unit's sergeant. Instead, I confided in another officer in our unit and shared the entire scenario with him in hopes of securing feedback on the next appropriate action. Alternatively, he shared the information with another member of our unit, and soon rumors began to spread.

Within a few days, I had FTO Eric visit me while covering a second shift at the Executive Residence. He stated he had "heard rumors around the department and knew he could trust me to tell the actual story." Instinctively, I asked him to tell me what he heard, and after hearing him report many of the major details, I foolishly verified his suspicions.

In that moment of sharing, I operated outside the trust of the Dignitary Unit and confided in a member of patrol. Since our unit was considered confidential, we were not union protected the same way patrol officers were. Unintentionally, I opened our select unit to scrutiny from within and from union backed patrol members at the same time. This act drove a wedge further between the Dignitary Unit and members of patrol, despite working for the same department.

Fearing the entire Dignitary Unit would face disciplinary action and potential dismissal, many individuals from the protection team ceased communication with me outside of work-related demands. Furthermore, DK7 continued to work while the department launched a private probe into workplace misconduct.

For weeks, I was alienated and harassed by various members of patrol seeking additional information regarding DK7's situation. Initially, the probes for information were relatively tame, generally consisting of patrol officers seeking updates they could share with their shift mates. When I refused to volunteer anything further, the general requests veered toward harassment.

Instead of focusing on DK7's transgressions, some patrol officers began to question my sexuality.

I was repeatedly asked about my sexual preference, called both fairy and faggot, and even questioned as to "why I would turn a good officer in for a little bit of porn" by a member of first shift patrol. The further I was pushed, the more I felt the need to defend my sexual preference.

The harassment became so ruthless that I opted for an overtly public engagement, in which I requested departmental permission to propose at the top of the capitol building overlooking the city. My rationale was that if patrol knew I was engaged, especially in the building that housed our police department, the persecution would stop. Just as I neared my breaking point, DK7 made a final flaw.

During the department's investigation, it was discovered that DK7 was identified purchasing pornographic material in a department issued polo bearing the Capitol Police name and embroidered badge. Evidently, he stopped at a gas station on his way into work and picked up a pornographic magazine to add to his collection. Generally, representing the department outside of work without prior authorization was frowned upon, but to do so while purchasing pornography was an extremely poor choice. Already under investigation, the timely complaint uncovered DK7's transgressions as a Capitol Police Officer. His hiding spot within the Executive Residence was raided and the pornography stash was unearthed. In a private exchange, he was allowed to collect his belongings and tenure his resignation. I witnessed DK7's final exit from the Executive Residence, which included a heartfelt handshake and goodbye from our unit's sergeant. While DK7 silently slipped through the iron gates, I remained trapped within.

Although the malevolent misogynist's reign had ended, the collateral damage surrounding his departure completely derailed my career. The position of protection I once revered developed into one I could not bear. DK7's sheltered investigation and quiet removal, coupled with the sexual harassment I endured, left me feeling dishonored.

I traded my integrity for a place in a game I had no idea how to play. Despite doing what I felt was right, I ended up feeling like a bad guy for blowing the whistle. Suddenly, I was trapped in a job I no longer loved.

I knew I had to escape, but circumstances would dictate that I remain a rat in an executive sized cage.

CHAPTER 11

PROTESTS AND POWERLIFTING

———

After the DK7 turmoil, I sought refuge in the gym.

As the Executive Residence remained hostile, spending time among the iron was the only environment in which I felt comfortable. While I was moving weight, nothing else mattered. Like pressing a mute button, I would silence the scrutinizing voices in my head and focus solely on maximizing each muscle contraction as I counted repetitions. Then, as I neared the point of failure, I would recall the most spiteful comments to fuel the final repetition.

Words like "faggot and fairy" fueled me to lift heavier.

At times, I even paired the belittling remarks with a mental image of the head of my oppressor slowly being crushed as I completed the lift. Twisted, yet effective, the mental imagery propelled me toward personal bests in every major lift. Suddenly, I found myself in a therapeutic relationship where goals were measured by pounds and muscle circumference. The heavier I lifted, the more my body grew to match the burden. As I grew, so did my desire to compete against other lifters.

Craving even more from my cast iron mistress, I entered my first powerlifting competition on March 27, 2010. The annual weightlifting competition was held on Milwaukee's blue collar southside at Kosciuszko Community Center. Lifters from the greater Milwaukee area, as well as neighboring states, showed up to compete at the event. The contest included bench press and deadlift for men and women, with trophies, medals, and an overall best lifter award.

Although I did not finish in the top three, I did place 10th in RAW bench press for males 181 lbs. and over, and a respectable 5th in assisted bench press for the same weight category. Given that I had not been training specifically for powerlifting, I knew my body was capable of much more.

Over the next year, I became completely infatuated with powerlifting. To become a legitimate contender, however, I needed to acquire a sponsor.

After months of internet searches for potential sponsors, I procured subsidies from an uprising supplement company, USPLabs. My sponsorship began with a giant box of supplements and two USPLabs t-shirts to wear while I worked out. Pumping my body full of a variety of chemicals in hopes of gaining a competitive edge, I consumed everything USPLabs sent me. Each supplement was considered legal at the time, including a now controversial compound known as DMAA.

It wasn't until 2016, that the FDA caught up with USPLabs and filed an 11-count grand jury indictment against the company. During my up rise in powerlifting, however, USPLabs promptly emerged as a top supplement distributor, making roughly 400 million dollars over a five-year period beginning in 2008.

With USPLabs in my corner, and their sketchy supplements coursing through my veins, I competed in four additional sanctioned powerlifting contests from 2010 to 2011. Each contest resulted in better outcomes, and I quickly climbed the ranks of Wisconsin's powerlifting elite. While I lived in the gym outside of work, things at work were also changing. The highly contested race for Wisconsin's 45th governor was underway, and our unit was guaranteed to receive a new leader in 2011.

Republican candidate Scott Walker was rumored to be looking to replace members of the Capitol Police with those of the Wisconsin State Patrol, should he win the election. This made tensions among the Dignitary Protection Unit even higher. Senior officers such as my sergeant, were habitually contacting human resources and obtaining retirement data.

Decades from retirement, I began to search the Wisconsin Government Job Site for employment alternatives. Eventually, I decided to apply for an opening with UW-Madison Police Department (UWPD) to serve as a Security Supervisor. However, the process to transfer and promote was extensive, and it would take months for a decision to be made.

As I waited to hear back from UWPD, Scott Walker was elected governor and inaugurated into office.

Shortly after his inauguration in 2011, Governor Walker introduced the controversial Wisconsin Act 10, also known as the Wisconsin Budget Repair Bill. In short, legislation was proposed to address a $3.6 billion budget deficit through targeting the public sector and collective bargaining. The bill, which aimed to eliminate collective bargaining for most of Wisconsin's public employees, gained national attention. In response, protesters flocked to the state capitol building in an unprecedented magnitude.

According to former Wisconsin Capitol Police Chief Charles Tubbs, "An estimated 1.5 million people visited the state capitol during 37 days of intense protests," (Tubbs, 2021). Chief Tubbs added, "the scale of the protests was evident considering the necessity for extensive external support, including 225 law enforcement agencies and a daily contingency of up to 550 officers," (Tubbs, 2021)

Throughout the protests, I was assigned to a logistics team operating out of the capitol building. The primary objective of our team was to ensure the officers working crowd control had the tools necessary to perform their duties. One of the greatest daily hurdles the logistics team faced was keeping the 500 plus officers fed and hydrated.

Being the largest member of the logistics team and able to move the most weight, I was relegated to the "cooler duty." This meant keeping over a dozen 120-quart coolers stocked with various beverages, along with food items, typically cold subs, for the officers to consume. To keep up with the demand for food and drink, I constantly rotated coolers and supplies by way of pushcart to various substations set up throughout the capitol.

Physically, the work was grueling. Densely packed crowds of protesters made moving items from one location to the next extremely difficult. At one point in time, I had a full soda can thrown at my head. The crowd, which was peaceful most of the time, typically refrained from such actions. After nearly being pegged by the can, however, I became more vigilant during the restock rounds.

Approximately three weeks into the nonstop sit-in protests, I injured my back while offloading one of the full coolers, which weighed almost 250 pounds. Instead of reporting the back injury, I ignored pain and opted to work through the discomfort. After suffering in silence for nearly a week, I finally went to a walk-in clinic on a precious day off.

At the clinic, I was informed that I had a "significant bulge" in my lower back, specifically between the L4 and L5 discs. I was cautioned against any unnecessary lifting or repetitive motion and instructed to set up an appointment with my primary care doctor to obtain a referral to a specialist.

In the meantime, I was provided a trio of medications to help with the radiating pain and debilitating sciatica I felt down the left side of my body. The concoction the walk-in doctor prescribed was Etodolac to help reduce inflammation, Tramadol for pain mitigation, and a muscle relaxant for the spasms. Initially, I was given a 90-day supply of each medication, after I described intense working conditions and inability to take time off to see my primary physician.

At the time of the injury, the protests completely consumed my schedule.

Meanwhile, I disregarded the doctor's orders and continued to push myself in the gym. Despite the back injury and sciatic nerve pain, I implemented a powerlifting centric based workout routine and continued to make gains. Everything I did was geared toward gradual weight increases and the overall goal of moving more weight.

My target date, which was set for July 12, 2011, was the Midwest Regional World Association of Benchers and Deadlifters (WABDL) Open Powerlifting Competition. Not only did I aim to compete at the regional open, but I also held every intention of setting the Wisconsin state record for the law enforcement and fire division contending in RAW bench press at 198 pounds.

I believed that if I could simply survive the injury until the competition, I would have ample time to recover before the WABDL World Championships held in November. Little did I know the ensuing price I would have to pay for my selfish ambitions and arrogance in the months that followed.

CHAPTER 12

TROPHIES

2011 was a year of collecting trophies.

Shortly after the capitol protests ended, I settled into a new position as Security Supervisor with the University of Wisconsin Police Department. With the change in position came a change in pay, and I began the process of building my first home.

On top of home building, I set a date in mid-September to marry my future trophy wife. There was also the rapidly approaching WABDL Midwest Regional, for which I continued to train daily.

In essence, I had a handful of major life events all set to occur within a couple of months. Survive it all, and I would have a comfortable place to display all the things I worked so hard to collect.

However, the more I added to my adult-sized plate, the more my anxiety grew to meet the burden. Aside from the prescribed anti-anxiety medication I was already taking, the only true coping strategy I had for the constant state of discomfort was the gym.

Managing the manic state of my life, with the expectations of a new career, all while training to win the Midwest

Regional with a severe back injury was proving to be too much. Instead of admitting defeat, I did what any reasonable person struggling with a misdiagnosed mental illness would do in the moment—I self-medicated and continued pushing forward. Similar to the facade my father maintained as principal, I strove to appear as if nothing was bothering me.

On the surface, I was the archetypal white male, grinding his way toward middle class existence. In actuality, I was about to run out of refills on the trifecta of medication that was keeping me afloat. I needed an immediate alternative.

After a bit of doctor shopping, I walked into an urgent care clinic that was not affiliated with my primary care doctor's network. Once in the clinic, I explained my sciatica and after a bit of manipulation, was prescribed thirty days' worth of Oxycontin. At the time, the medication seemed to be the answer to my prayers.

Over the next month, I paired the pain medication with a plethora of under-regulated USPLabs supplements. As I continued to train for the regional, I maintained the impression of being well by continuing to attend my 9 to 5 and volunteering to work overtime events.

I recall working Safety Saturday, a collaborative agency event held on June 11th, 2011, geared toward educating parents and children on ways to make safe decisions. It was abnormally hot outside, and I was dressed as McGruff the Crime Dog. As I posed for photos with children and their families, sweat saturated my body. It was easily 15 degrees warmer inside the canine costume. On top of the extreme heat, each photo op tested my pain tolerance, as I constantly knelt to greet the small children. Every time I repositioned myself, my back responded with shooting pain.

Fortunately, the McGruff mascot head hid all signs of discomfort. In most regards, working the sweltering event was easier than my daily routine, because the outfit served as the disguise I typically had to create. With the Midwest Regional less than a month away, I continued to ignore my body and live in my iron sanctuary.

Then, roughly two weeks to the competition, I ran out of Oxycontin. Fortunately, I was able to procure a single refill, as the prescription was not nearly as regulated in 2011 as pain medication is today.

Next, I divided the thirty-day supply into two containers: one for each week leading up to the competition. My methodology was that I could double the allotted dosage of pain meds, from two to four pills per day, and have just enough to sustain me through the day of the competition. I certainly wasn't happy about having to ration my pill supply, but it was the only working alternative I could think of, while still maintaining what I considered to be an effective dose.

With the medication situation temporarily sorted, I felt comfortable enough to turn my focus back to powerlifting. I spent the next week performing the opening lifts I would need to hit on competition day. While doing so, I re-aggravated the L4 and L5 disc injury to the point that I could not bend over to remove or even tie my own shoes.

Despite the debilitating pain, I remained determined to compete in at least one major lifting category at the Midwest Regional.

With my back spasms returning in full force, competing in the dead lift no longer seemed to be a viable option. On the evening prior to the competition, I opted to remove myself from the dead lift event to focus solely on the RAW bench press in the Law Enforcement Fire Division. If I were to remain in contention to participate at World's, I would have to set the Wisconsin State record for RAW bench press in my division at 198 pounds.

On July 12, 2011, I checked in at the Crowne Plaza Hotel in Madison, WI and proceeded directly to weigh-ins. After making weight at 197.5 pounds, I found an unoccupied corner of a hotel conference room that had been converted to a lifter's warm-up area. Once settled, I positioned myself as comfortably as possible in a hard-plastic chair and awaited the announcement for lifting events and order of appearance.

After waiting for what seemed like an eternity, I found out that I was the only individual competing in the Law Enforcement-Fire Division. This meant that I would be lifting alone and have nobody but myself to propel me toward victory. Where most competitors may have found this awkward, I found comfort in the solitude. After all, I was accustomed to confronting situations on my own.

Once it was finally my turn to lift, I immediately found my element. I cracked open a fresh bottle of Nose Tork, a popular ammonia based smelling salt, and instantly woke my body up.

As I positioned myself on the weight bench, I suddenly felt a string of spasms lighting up the pain receptors in my lower back like an arcade game. Despite the warning signs, I unracked the opening weight of 142 kilos. Under the added weight, my back muscles screamed out, only to be drowned out by a "press" command. With relative ease, I bench pressed the weight and completed the opener. Next, I jumped the weight to 150 kilos/330 pounds and eleven ounces. This was enough to capture the Wisconsin State record in my division, which was previously set at 148 kilos/326 pounds.

After a brief hiatus, I took another hit of Nose Tork and was back on the bench.

Instant spasms!

My body was literally crying out for me to stop; however, I would not concede. I unracked the weight and slowly let it descend to my chest until the "press" command set me free. With every ounce of effort, I exploded through the weight and pressed it toward the ceiling. It wasn't until after I heard the crowd cheer and the lifting referee yell "rack it" that I knew I completed the lift. Only this time, I struggled as I transitioned to sit up.

As I labored to get back to my feet, I briefly exchanged words with the lifting referee. In a concerned voice he stated, "I heard a pop." I responded with a shrug, and nonchalantly noted, "my back is fucked." At that moment, I should have stopped and celebrated my accomplishment. Instead, I chose to jump the weight another five kilos to 155 kilos. When healthy, I knew I could push 400 pounds, so I was determined to hit as close to that mark as possible.

The result of my final lift was not what I desired. Shortly after receiving the "press" command, I began to drive the weight from my chest. Only this time, the 341 pounds I was lifting stalled out. As the weight was about to come crashing down on me, I was saved by two spotters and a third individual pulled from the crowd.

Like a true champion, I thought to myself, I left everything on the floor. Little did I know, everything was about to become an understatement.

CHAPTER 13

TOO MUCH

———

After securing the state record at WABDL Midwest Regional, I should have celebrated the outcome and taken ample time to recover. Instead, I plummeted into a deep state of depression. Despite the victory, my mood swung from manic high to depressive low.

A past counselor compared the volatility of my mental health to a roller coaster, which served as an accurate portrayal. Like riding a giant drop, experiencing such an intense build up to the competition only made the subsequent plunge afterward that much more severe. Pair mental instability with an addiction to painkillers, and in a short time span you have created the recipe for personal disaster.

When I could no longer legally obtain refills on the Oxycontin, I began to substitute other pain medications in its place. First, I drank a leftover bottle of cough syrup that contained codeine from our medicine cabinet. When my soon-to-be wife realized the bottle was missing, I made up a lie that cat had knocked it over and spilled it to cover my tracks.

I witnessed my father lying to conceal his addiction countless times. I was so used to it that I was barely aware I began doing it myself. Lies began to build on top of one another, making it difficult to decipher between fact and fiction.

Once the cough syrup was empty, I transitioned to Phenylbutazone (bute), a non-steroidal anti-inflammatory drug (NSAID) used to treat pain and inflammation in horses. I remember using 1/8 the dosage that was prescribed to my fiancé's horse and allowing the bitter oral paste to dissolve under my tongue. Over time, I began pairing the horse bute with alcohol to help curb the disgusting taste. Since the drug required a veterinarian's prescription, I was again working with a limited supply. At the time, I was so addicted to taking something for the pain, that I used to dumpster dive at the barn, hoping to find remnants of bute tubes or similar NSAIDs to consume. On evenings where I could not find any pain-relieving drug to take, I begrudgingly settled for the combination of hard liquor and Trazodone, a popular antidepressant and sedative.

Despite whatever concoction I derived, nothing alleviated the physical pain and mental anxiety the way Oxycontin did. Ultimately, I knew that I needed an alternative drug solution and began canvasing the gym for potential suppliers.

Roughly a few weeks before my first wedding in September 2011, I found an individual through the gym that was able to solve my supply issue. For only three dollars per pill, he was able to get me a veterinary grade alternative to Oxycontin shipped directly from Canada. The catch, or so he said, was "you had to order a minimum of 200 pills because the distributor only dealt in bulk."

The addict in me knew that quantity would not be an issue, and I promptly placed an order for 200 pills. My intent was to purchase more, but not until after I sampled the product. My back pain was so unmanageable, I was struggling to complete any tasks that required bending over. Even dressing myself for work became nearly impossible. Thinking I found a long-term pain solution to supplement my drug of choice made me nearly euphoric.

Unfortunately, I did not have an additional 600 dollars to spend on pills prior to a wedding I was already struggling to afford. I also did not have anyone in my life that I trusted enough to talk to about my spiraling addiction or ask for a "no questions asked" loan. Instead, I sold a gaming system along with a prized lot of vintage Star Wars toys to cover the costs. It was difficult to let go of the childhood possessions, but in the moment, I needed the pills more.

The allotment of 200 pills I received should have lasted three months, at the rate of two pills a day. However, after I was able to sample the product, I realized the potency was not equivalent to the Oxycontin in effect or duration. This led to me starting each day by crushing one pill to snort, while I consumed another orally. The fix would last three to four hours and by noon, I was repeating the process. Soon, I began experiencing side effects from taking the veterinary grade medication.

One of the biggest aftereffects from taking the medication was chronic fatigue. I was tired all the time.

To counteract the drowsiness, I began consuming USPLabs Jack3d pre-workout powder mixed into energy drinks throughout the day. The overall combination provided just enough functionality to where I could perform my job as a Security Supervisor and still satisfy my need as an opioid addict. As the workday dragged on, I resorted to taking four more pills. Two pills were consumed at lunch and another two prior to leaving for the day. This occurred sometime between 3 p.m. and 4 p.m.

After work, I would recharge with another round of pre-workout powder combined with an energy drink, about fifteen minutes prior to heading to the gym. Finally, after a one to two hour lifting session to maintain my physique, I would head home to eat and relax for the evening. On most nights, I continued to chase the prescription Trazodone with a shot of whatever alcohol was available to ensure a few hours of quality sleep.

I stayed locked in this cycle of polysubstance abuse well past the day of my September wedding.

Before I realized it, a month had passed, and I consumed nearly all 200 pills from my initial purchase. I called my dealer, who doubled as an occasional lifting partner, and told him I was going to need to re-up sooner than expected. Jon, as we will call him, didn't immediately hit me back. Instead, I waited for what seemed like an eternity to place my order. Then, one Saturday morning in early October, Jon called me back. Only this time, it wasn't pills that he had to offer.

CHAPTER 14

CHAINS THAT BIND US

I just missed a phone call from an individual named Jon. Jon, a man of many hats, typically called me for one of two reasons. The first was to see when I would be hitting the gym for a lift. The second, was to see when I would be hitting the gym so we could discuss business. Either way, a call from Jon habitually resulted in a trip to the gym. This call, however, was immediately different in that it was accompanied by a voicemail.

"A voicemail," I mumbled to myself as I searched the kitchen for something to eat. I thought we agreed to never leave voicemails unless it was dire or an absolute emergency. I became accustomed to receiving short, cryptic texts from Jon, but never a voicemail. My mind immediately jumped to the worst-case scenario. "Had Jon been busted?" Bypassing the thought of breakfast completely, I sprinted back upstairs to check the voicemail.

"Hey Travis, this is Jon, we workout together at the Princeton Club sometimes and I remember you telling me you like dogs." A brief pause. "Anyway, I know this house where they have a dog, looks like a Pitbull or something, outside chained to a tree. They don't seem to give a shit about it, and

I thought you might want to check it out." Another extended pause. "If you text me, I'll send you the address... and if you are interested, better hurry bro, I'm not sure how much longer the dog will be there."

I hung up the phone and pondered to myself. We already had one dog in the house along with two cats. However, both cats belonged to my wife and came with the marriage. Our dog, Bonsai, had also become bonded to my wife and frequently served as her barn companion when she went to ride her horse. Perhaps it was mania, or the need for companionship of my own, that drove me to text Jon back. Send me the address and I'll check it out.

As I waited for Jon's return text, I threw on some clothes and got ready to head out the door. I stuffed a backpack full of treats, as well as one of Bonsai's backup leashes, just in case I decided to bring the animal home. While I waited, I prospected as to what kind of dog it was. Was it male or female, would the owner(s) simply give it away or would I need money? I had so many questions and no immediate answers, until my phone chimed again. Jon responded with a short text containing a remote address, somewhere near Stoughton, WI, a small city about twenty miles southeast from Madison.

On my way out the door, I briefly contemplated calling my wife and alerting her to the situation. However, I knew she would immediately say no to bringing another animal into the house, especially seeing how we already had three pets at home. Instead, I opted for the act now and apologize later approach. After a brief stop for gas and a fast-food drive-thru lunch, I was on the road to Stoughton.

Like much of rural Wisconsin, this area was divided by acres of farm fields with the occasional house. As I closed in on the county road address, I realized I was likely looking for a farmhouse or something similar. With less than a mile to my destination according to the GPS, I could see a giant oak tree silhouetted against the early afternoon sun. As the oak tree became clearer, so did a long gravel driveway, lined with vehicles in various states of disrepair, leading up to a partially painted, dilapidated older home.

The GPS called out, "Your destination is ahead on the right," and I steered the car up the driveway toward the house. In the distance, I began to make out the shape of a small animal, possibly a dog, lying underneath the ancient tree.

Instead of proceeding directly to the house, I stopped mid-driveway to take further inventory of the entire situation. Without realizing it at first, I found myself falling back on my police training. After assessing the situation for safety, I turned my attention to the dog and the beautiful brindle markings among its patchwork coat. They reminded me of a tiger shark with the way the sun glistened off the symmetrical stripes of alternating caramel and black fur.

As I examined further, I noted ribs protruding from both sides of the body, coupled with a visible spinal column peeking through the layers of dermis. Even more disturbing, was the heavy gauge chain that was secured with a padlock tight around the dog's scab riddled neck. An empty metal dish, which should have contained water, lay upside down in the dirt nearby. The emaciated animal did not even lift its head when I opened the car door to move in for a closer view.

A secondary assessment revealed additional areas of major concern. The dog's front legs were coated from forearm to foot with what appeared to be dried blood. The ears were also badly serrated, as if they were roughly cut with some scissors, or shredded by the claws of a feral cat. The tail was docked, or deliberately cut off, but in a way that looked improper and too long for a skilled veterinarian.

As I inched closer to determine the sex, I heard a low growl begin to resonate. Fearful, but not discouraged, I retreated to the car for the backpack full of treats. As I withdrew, the dog rose, providing a full view of its body for the first time. "It" was now determined to be she, and she was broken just like me.

I tossed a handful of treats in her direction and continued up the driveway to the front door of the house. I tried the doorbell, which didn't seem to work, then proceeded to pound on the closed door. I knocked until my knuckles were beat red, but nobody responded. Through the door I yelled, "I'm interested in your dog." Still nothing.

"I have money."

Again nothing. Finally, as I was about to walk back to the car, I saw a finger pull down a section of broken blinds to look outside.

Once more, I yelled, "I'm interested in your dog, the starving one chained to the tree out front. What do you want for her?"

After what seemed like an eternity of silence with no response, I walked back to the car and considered what to do next.

When I walked past her on my way to the car, I noticed she ate all the treats that were within chain's length. I grabbed another handful and threw them in her direction as I got into my vehicle. I sat there and watched her eat, realizing that this dog would die if I didn't do something.

As I put the car in reverse, I began to cry, knowing that by leaving I had sealed her fate. I consulted the GPS for directions and began to drive. Only my next intended stop wasn't home, it was to a hardware store that I had passed along the way.

At the hardware store, I made two purchases; The largest bolt cutter they had in stock, along with an oversized beach towel that was left over from summer clearance. I planned to use the bolt cutter on the pad lock, while the towel was going to be used to swaddle the dog and hopefully load her into the car. I drove back to the house and proceeded directly to the front door. Again, I knocked until my knuckle's turned blood red, and again nobody answered. I shouted through the door, "I'm taking your dog!"

Next, I headed back to the tree where she was chained.

As opposed to cutting the lock, which would ultimately free the dog completely, I focused my attention on the chain. As I distracted her with the remaining dog treats, I proceeded to the opposite side of the tree to work on the chain. At first, the bolt cutter did not penetrate the thick link of the chain. However, I was able to utilize the tree's trunk as a base for one of the arms of the bolt cutter and depress the other arm in a bench press type motion. By maximizing the leverage in such a manner, I relieved some of the pressure on my ailing back and allowed the bolt cutter to make light work of the chain. Next, I utilized the chain as a leash and tried to walk her to the car. This failed miserably, as she immediately resisted the makeshift leash.

For ages, we remained in a standoff. I would attempt to pull her closer to the vehicle with the chain, and she would put on the brakes. I would exert myself further, only to be betrayed by back spasms.

After what seemed like hours, I was finally able to coax her into the backseat of the vehicle with the remaining french fries from my fast-food lunch. Although she growled at me at least a dozen times, she never bit me, which I considered a good sign. As we traveled together, she laid curled in a tight ball, awake and constantly vigilant of my movements. I kept an eye on her and positioned the rearview mirror in a manner that I could see her the entire journey. Trust was something that would have to be built with time, but for the moment, she was safe.

As we got closer to home, I tried to figure out how I was going to introduce her to my wife. I settled upon a half-truth and decided to run with the story that I got her from a guy at the gym who was struggling to take care of her. In doing so, I also realized that she was going to need a name.

Given the situation from which she was just rescued from, her name needed to be something strong. Since she looked like she might be a Boxer, and was certainly a fighter, I was gravitating toward the name Ali. However, Ali was clearly a male's name and I needed something a touch more feminine.

With the car parked in the garage, I went to immediately remove her from the backseat, and she snapped at me. It was a cautionary bite, aimed to correct my behavior, but not harm me. In my haste, I had nearly forgotten the broken situation from which she had just come. I needed to take things slow. Karma had almost come back to bite me and in that moment, I immediately knew her name.

"I'm going to name you Karma," I told her, as if she would recognize the new name. "Now wait here, while I explain how you came to be."

CHAPTER 15

BREAKING CHAINS

——

Karma spent her first night at the house sleeping in the garage. It certainly wasn't ideal, but I did my best to make her comfortable providing ample blankets, access to fresh water and a space heater just in case the temperature dropped. Honestly, I would have been joining her in the garage had my wife had her way.

"There is no way that filthy creature is coming into the house!" my wife's words echoed in my head as I grabbed a pillow from the master bedroom. Like Karma, I was also banished; my resting place was a futon in the spare bedroom. "And don't even think about introducing her to Bonsai until she has seen a vet," were the last words I heard before laying down for the evening. "Well worth the price of saving an animal's life," I muttered to myself as I tried to find comfort on the thin futon mattress.

As hours passed, I laid awake making a mental list of everything Karma would need before I could attempt to assimilate her into our home. Like most rescue animals, she needed a lot of attention.

First, we would have to make a vet visit. When I unloaded her from the car, I noticed she left behind some tiny insect passengers, which I assumed were fleas. In addition to the likelihood of parasites, the exposed wounds on her ears, forelegs and around her neck would require immediate attention. I also made a mental note to check her teeth, as they were barely visible when she attempted to snap at me earlier in the evening. Finally, as I was making the list for Karma, I realized I was scraping the bottom of the barrel on my pain meds. I needed to contact Jon to restock; he might also have some idea of what Karma had been through.

The next morning, I woke up and immediately texted Jon that we needed to meet for a "workout session." While I waited for his return text, I went to the garage to check on Karma. "Shit! I forgot to remove your padlock and chain," I apologized to the now alert animal staring back at me. Between the fight with my wife and the dwindling supply of pain medication, my mind was distracted at best. "Time to concentrate on removing this chain," I said out loud as I closed the distance between us.

I was a few feet away when Karma let out a low growl. "So, you're going to make this difficult... well let me at least take you outside to go potty." Again, I utilized the chain as a leash and secured a solid grasp on the final few links before opening the garage door. To my surprise, Karma did not bolt immediately upon seeing daylight. Instead, she slowly sauntered toward the sunlight and then made a beeline for the grass. This is progress, I thought to myself, while I continued to examine her at chain length.

Once the bathroom break concluded, I eventually coaxed her back into the garage by pretending I had a treat. Clearly, Karma was food motivated and I made another mental note to purchase more dog treats later that afternoon. I was just about to grab the bolt cutter from the car when I received a return text from Jon.

"Princeton Club East, 1 p.m.," was all the text read.

Like a teenager who just received a text from a crush, I immediately replied, "See you there!" I recall feeling exhilarated, thinking that Jon was going to be able to provide the answers I needed regarding Karma, along with the pain medication that was keeping me afloat. Again, I turned my attention to the chain.

If I could only get close enough with the bolt cutter, I knew I could make light work of the generic padlock. Utilizing what I just discovered about Karma being food motivated, I decided to get a bowl of Bonsai's dog food to distract her. As Karma ate, I crept toward her with the bolt cutter, until I was within inches of the lock.

Moving slowly, I engaged the bolt cutter around the lock and immediately squeezed the handles. The lock shank cracked under the pressure, drawing Karma's attention away from the food. A long, drawn-out warning growl alerted me I only had a few seconds to fully remove the chain from around her neck. While doing so, I exposed even more damaged skin coupled with bloody sores that retained an embedded chain link pattern. Now I better understood Karma's distress.

"You have been through absolute hell, my dear," I told her as I dragged the chain over to the recycling bin. Tears filled my eyes as I said, "Try to get some rest and I'll be back in a couple hours."

While Karma recuperated in the garage, I transitioned from collected caregiver into intense powerlifter. I changed roles with such frequency during those days, that I felt like two or three separate people sharing one body. With each unique situation I entered, I presented a different variation of my personality. The next few hours required a tougher, more street savvy version of myself and I intended to play the part with conviction.

As I passed a mirror in the hallway, I barely recognized my own reflection. My hair was a mess from sleeping on the futon, I had blood on my shirt from Karma's wounds, and it had been a few days since my last shower. Instead of heading out to meet Jon right away, I took a few minutes to put myself together. After all, I refused to look desperate in front of him, or anybody else. Thirty minutes later, I pulled into the parking lot and saw Jon's tinted BMW rolling in behind me.

We remained in the lot and talked from one vehicle to another. I explained to Jon how I acquired Karma and asked again if he had any additional information. He told me he really didn't know anything else about her, except that, "she might have been used for fighting practice for a couple of the other dogs." Then, as if he were working on commission, Jon promptly transitioned to business.

He asked if I'd be interested in some Vicodin to "tie me over until he could get in another order of the vet grade stuff." I immediately jumped at the opportunity and dropped three hundred dollars on thirty pills. Jon and I both knew the price point didn't matter. I would have paid any dollar amount at this point; I was so desperate to feed my addiction. Jon couldn't have known how hard up I was, but he had been dealing long enough to know that I was closing in on desperation. Perhaps my facade as the street-smart tough guy wasn't as convincing as I thought.

After paying Jon, he told me we could re-up again in a couple weeks. Constantly calculating, that meant I could take two Vicodin per day and supplement with the remainder of the vet grade pain meds as needed. It also meant that I had two weeks to come up with an additional six hundred dollars, plus whatever Karma's vet bills were about total in the upcoming week. I immediately knew I needed to come up with additional funds and fast.

Time would quickly reveal how far I was willing to go to feed my addiction, along with the latest addition to our home.

CHAPTER 16

FROM COP TO CRIMINAL

———

A day after I spoke with Jon, on October 12, Karma was taken to her first vet appointment. With the assistance of two well trained veterinary technicians, we were able to obtain her weight along with an estimated age. Karma weighed in at a meager 37 pounds and was determined to be approximately one year old based on her size and dental examination. Her age was a rough estimation however, due primarily to the fact that many of her teeth had been damaged from "excessively chewing on a hard or improper object(s)."

The fucking chain I thought to myself, as we waited to see the veterinarian.

I immediately knew I made the right choice of vets when Dr. Kristi entered the examination room with a variety of distraction treats. I made note of Karma's situation on the pre-examination forms but wasn't sure how the vet would respond. While Karma enjoyed licking liverwurst from a tongue depressor, Dr. Kristi cautiously began to assess her.

The good doctor immediately informed me that Karma had Demodectic Mange, or microscopic mites, that were causing the scaly bald patches. Further inspection revealed that Karma's front dew claws had been improperly removed, likely by pliers, and were now badly infected. It wasn't all bad news, however. Despite her tail being docked incorrectly, it had "healed nicely." After another helping of liverwurst, Dr. Kristi listened to Karma's heart and discovered a slight murmur. An ultrasound was recommended to evaluate the severity of the murmur, along with the possible source. Finally, the serrated cuts in both of Karma's ears appeared to be the work of cat claws and would ultimately need to be docked to prevent further splitting and future damage.

Dr. Krisit's overall assessment was that Karma was severely malnourished, roughly 20 pounds underweight for her estimated age, and in need of medical intervention to increase her chances of survival.

Given that it was a rescue situation, the doctor agreed to "work with me on costs" while projecting a minimum of "2,000 dollars to bring the animal back to health." I intuitively knew I could not afford anywhere near 2,000 dollars but agreed to work with the doctor anyway to help ensure Karma's survival.

After rescuing her from being chained to a tree, I simply wouldn't allow her to perish over money. I became attached to her so quickly and her fighter's spirit encouraged me that she could make a comeback. Even though I needed the money for meds, I would have paid anything to give her a chance.

Once I signed a textbook sized pile of paperwork, it was agreed that Karma would stay in the veterinarian's care for two nights. During that time, she would be stabilized with fluids, undergo a canine spay procedure, and have the outstanding issues with her teeth, dew claws, and ears addressed. Furthermore, Karma's vaccinations would be updated, and a combination of antibiotics included in her regimen to fight off the mites. Overall, the level of care she would be receiving seemed well worth the projected costs.

As Karma was recovering in the veterinarian's office, I spent the next two days figuring out how I was going to raise the 2,000 dollars for her treatments. First thing I did was sell what remained of my father's coin collection to a local pawn shop. The variety of gold and silver coins netted 800 dollars. Next, I took my original Nintendo gaming system along with approximately thirty games to a video game exchange store. I was elated when the owner discovered a few rare vintage games and offered me 600 dollars for the bundle. A phone call to my mother, an avid dog lover, resulted in a 300 dollar check which I drove an hour and a half to pick up.

With 1,700 dollars raised, I remember feeling unstoppable. Nothing in the world could prevent me from raising an additional 300 dollars and reaching my goal. Then, I remembered that I still need 600 dollars to cover "the medication" that I ordered through Jon. Like a roller coaster, my emotional high plummeted into a depressive low. I could not see a path in which I could pay for Karma's surgery as well as the need to feed my addiction.

Like most of the other hardships I faced in life, I took it upon myself to secure the money by any means possible. I was willing to sacrifice anything, including my remaining morals, to come up with the funds. I even considered robbing Jon, knowing that a drug dealer was unlikely to report a crime. This all-in mentality, coupled with the relentless need to consume a pill to feel normal, led me down a path where I began stealing.

From October 2011, until I was eventually arrested in June 2012, I stole credit card data along with an individual's personal information on six separate occasions. Each act of theft resulted in two Class A Misdemeanor charges: one for theft of movable-property and another for false representation. At the time, I rationalized the thefts to maintain the vicious cycle of opioid addiction of which I was locked. I refused to formally recognize my addiction and continually lied to myself and those around me. Eventually, all the lies came crashing down.

One life lesson recovery has taught me is that being honest, no matter how shameful the act, is the only avenue to receiving the support one needs to recover. As opposed to telling a lie, or omitting pieces of my story, I want to reiterate a well-known fact about individuals struggling with active addiction.

The compulsion to use drugs may lead some individuals to steal to obtain money for those drugs. While I am in no way justifying the act of theft to acquire drugs or other illegal substances, I feel it is important to identify the connection between the two.

For me, an abusive childhood, a job that took advantage of my willingness to help others, a position as a cop who saw the darker side of police enforcement and so on led me to the point where I was willing to steal to make ends meet. After seeing others in positions of power commit overt travesties, I no longer cared about what was deemed morally right. Instead, I was willing to do anything to feed the needs of my addiction. This included sacrificing anything and everything in my life, as I violated my personal beliefs to feed an insatiable opioid appetite.

As my life with Karma was just about to begin, everything that came before it was literally falling to pieces.

CHAPTER 17

HIGH FUNCTIONING ADDICT

———

Karma and I grew together over the next year. The more time I invested into returning her to health, the more she began to trust me. With each interaction, the two of us became more comfortable showing each other our true natures. In the first month of Karma being home, I learned more about her character than anything else. As the wounds from her previous owner healed, she began to show signs of becoming the loving companion that every man yearns to discover. Initially, her love allowed me to touch her without any recoil or negative reaction.

Once I was able to touch Karma, I began training her. At first, this meant putting a slip leash around her neck without any aggression. We practiced putting the leash on and taking it off every day for almost two months before moving on to the next breakthrough.

My goal was to get her comfortable with the actions surrounding the leash, especially my hands traveling above or around her head. Like most abused animals, Karma was head shy, and would immediately duck away when a hand was extended toward her. Only through repetition and positive reinforcement, was I able to demonstrate to Karma that I was safe and posed no threat of violent behavior. Next, came the more difficult task of training Karma to walk on the leash.

Having grown up with Greater Swiss Mountain dogs, a powerful draft breed, I knew from experience that dogs could generate a great deal of force at the end of a leash. Karma was no exception. Our first walks together consisted of her pulling my two hundred plus pound frame in any direction she saw fit. Despite being underweight, Karma possessed the strength and drive of a champion puller. For the sake of my rotator cuffs, I needed to develop an approach to walking her where I maintained control of our pace and direction of travel.

By chance, I was up late one evening and caught an episode of Cesar Millan, where he was retraining a pit bull with similar tendencies. Utilizing Cesar's leash training methods on Karma, I was able to convert her into an acceptable walker with a few months practice.

After leash training and the acquisition of a few basic commands, I decided Karma needed some additional form of socialization in her life. Bonsai, our Goldendoodle, was already attending an award-winning dog day camp and it was time that Karma joined him. I still recall blatantly lying on the dog behavioral section to ensure she would be admitted. I certainly couldn't write, "was used as a potential bait dog, but currently shows no signs of aggression." Instead, I opted for "plays well with Bonsai in our backyard."

On Karma's first day of camp, I experienced a level of anxiety that could only be rivaled by a parent leaving a child at daycare for the first time.

I spent the day neurotically checking my cell phone to ensure I hadn't missed a call or text. I simply wasn't sure how Karma would respond to an environment full of other dogs and alternative caregivers. To my delight, Karma completed her first day at Camp K9 without incident. More shockingly, she bonded with one of the camp counselors, and even allowed the girl to pet her throughout the day. While Karma discovered the pleasures of being a pampered dog at camp, I continued to provide UW-Madison with a warm body serving in the role of Security Supervisor.

Monday through Friday, I presented myself as an authoritative figure, while internally I leveraged the self-control of an unresponsive toddler. Outside of Karma and her training, my thoughts remained fixated upon the last time I used, and when I was going to use next. I was trapped in the cycle of addiction. Most of my days were merely an act upon the stage of life.

I faked everything and did so with an aptitude that could have placed me in contention to win an Academy Award. Even my police colleagues were convinced, and I was promoted from sharing a common workspace to having my own office.

"Out of sight, out of mind," became my mentality once I was isolated from the rest of the Infrastructure Security Unit. Since my primary duty was to oversee the campus's camera systems, along with providing security assessments for new construction projects on campus, I could be nearly anywhere on the 936-acre campus at any moment.

The flexibility of my position afforded ample opportunity for me to take pain medication while working without being detected.

I was also supplementing with a vast array of heavily caffeinated pre-workout products to help mask the side effects of the veterinary grade medication. Overall, I avoided interacting with my co-workers as much as possible, while completing enough work that I wouldn't be reprimanded.

To this day, I still don't understand how I managed to pull this off. My use went undetected for nearly a year and a half of employment. Given that most of my daily life from this period remains a drug-induced blur, I find it difficult to fathom that I was never questioned regarding my disguised behavior. I literally worked under the influence of an opioid every day in the presence of trained police officers and security professionals, and nobody said a thing.

Certainly, I must have slipped up at multiple points along the way prior to being arrested?

At my worst, I was snorting a crushed line of pain medication directly off my work desk prior to beginning my shift at 7 a.m. Between the never-ending runny nose, frequent sick calls, and erratic quantity and quality of my work, someone should have at least pegged me as a cokehead. Perhaps, growing up with an alcoholic father taught me to mask my addiction so well even those closest to me failed to see it?

Fortunately, the science surrounding addiction has come up with a phrase to describe such a phenomenon: high-functioning addict.

A high-functioning addict is an individual who appears to be perfectly fine on the exterior, while maintaining the compulsive need to consume their drug of choice. For example, I showed up for work because I knew I needed the biweekly check to support my drug habit. I no longer cared about the title or responsibility associated with my position but was driven to work because it provided the means to purchase the drugs I craved. If I kept working, I was able to maintain my addiction.

Today, most experts will agree that addiction has little to do with one's ability to keep their life in order. Instead, they view addiction as a chronic brain disease. The continual consumption of the drug of choice causes changes in an individual's brain chemistry, making it difficult for a user to control their impulses. The absence of impulse control, coupled with a substance that is addictive by nature, often renders users incapable of fighting the disease.

Add family history of alcohol abuse, plus an under diagnosed mental illness, and you begin to see my true struggles. However, it wasn't until the city police caught up with me at work in June 2012, that I began to see them for myself.

CHAPTER 18

UNDER ARREST

June 19, 2012, began like countless other days before it. I woke up, got ready for work, and drove the eight mile stretch from our home to campus. While most people have similar morning routines, I spent most of my morning fixated on how many drugs I needed to make it through the day. After parking my vehicle, I calculated my allotted rations, before heading into the UW-Police Department Infrastructure Security office. From that moment on, the day was anything but typical.

Immediately upon my arrival, I was told to report to my lieutenant's office. As I walked in, I quickly realized this wasn't a spur of the moment review or reprimand for forgetting paperwork; there were two city police officers and a plain clothes detective waiting in his office.

I could tell by their menacing looks that this wasn't a meet and greet either. Overall, I had a sinking feeling that they were there specifically for me, but I was too preoccupied with when I was going to be able to take my next dose of pain medication to care. Before I could act, my lieutenant instructed me to "take a seat."

My instinct was to run but I was already in a police sub-station, surrounded by officers with nowhere to go. As opposed to bolting out the door, I sat down, which was the only viable option given the totality of the circumstances. Next, came the inquisition.

As the plain clothes detective pressed me for information regarding stolen credit card data, I sat quietly, knowing she already had answers to many of her questions. While she talked, my mind remained fixated upon the pills in my car and how I would instantly decline a search if prompted. As the detective continued, I recalled what I learned from attending criminal law class at Lakeland College. In my head, I repeated the mantra "the police are not your friends." To me, this meant no matter what the detective offered, or how she claimed she could "help me if I cooperated," I needed to remain silent until I was in the presence of an attorney.

I also recalled the former District Attorney that taught the class saying, "the police can and will lie to you during an investigation; however, if you lie back to them, it can be considered obstruction of justice." Rather than tell the detective a bullshit story, I continued to sit in silence.

Once the frustrated investigator realized she was not going to coax any additional information from me, she instructed one of the officers to place me under arrest. This is where things got interesting.

Although I remained silent, I also remained compliant to the officer's commands.

As he instructed me to "stand up and face the wall," I did exactly what he directed. After patting me down for weapons or any other sharp objects, the officer read me my Miranda Rights, and placed me in cuffs. This was all standard procedure, until he powerfully squeezed each individual cuff tightly to my wrists.

According to *A Training Guide for Law Enforcement Officers*, printed May 3, 2007, the officer should have "used touch-pressure, and ratchetted the handcuffs closed." Next, the officer should have "checked the handcuffs for tightness, then safety-locked (double-locked) them." For those unfamiliar with handcuffs, applying the safety-lock ensures the handcuffs do not continue to tighten while the officer escorts and transports an individual. Neither of these steps were followed.

As the officer escorted me outside the security office and to his vehicle, I alerted him to the situation with my cuffs.

"Oh, so you want to talk now," the officer responded dismissively, as he roughly pushed me into the awaiting backseat of his car. Next, he went to fasten my seat belt and blatantly hard-pressed his forearm against the right side of my cheek. Again, this was an untrained technique as the officer should have "stabilized the subject's head and upper body with his forearm", while securing the seatbelt across my body. While the officer was stuffing me into the back of the police car, the handcuffs continued to tighten on both my wrists.

During the transport to jail, I again alerted the officer to the painful constriction of my handcuffs, which was now coupled with complete numbness in my right hand. Again, he ignored my complaint and continued to drive toward the jail as if I said nothing. I knew from my training in law enforcement that he should have been monitoring me during the drive. Instead, the officer decided to act against his training.

As a result, every bump and pothole the police vehicle hit caused my cuffs to ratchet tighter, until they could ratchet no further.

By the time we arrived at Dane County Jail, both my hands turned purple and were completely numb. Next, I sat in booking for what seemed like an eternity. Still in handcuffs while the officer completed the necessary paperwork, I began to worry about permanent nerve damage. I could no longer feel either of my hands and noticed blood coming from a "pinch point" and dripping down off my right pinky finger.

Sometime during the booking process, a jail deputy removed the handcuffs after noticing I was dripping blood on the floor. At that point, I had been in the cuffs for nearly an hour. Once the cuffs were removed, deep purple furrows revealed themselves along with broken skin at two contact points. The deep indentations left by the handcuffs reminded me of Karma's neckline after I removed the chain. The deputy gloved up and rendered aid to both wrists while I waited to complete the booking process. It was a cold exchange, but I was thankful to have my hands finally freed.

After being booked into Dane County Jail on misdemeanor theft charges, I was released until a preliminary hearing date was set a couple months down the road. Having spent the better portion of the day in jail, I needed to find a way back to my car and the pills stashed inside. Not ready to call my wife and explain why I needed a ride from jail back to the department, I opted to walk. As I walked, I continually flexed my hands in hopes feeling would return.

In the days that followed, my right wrist and hand continued to lose feeling sporadically throughout the day. I was also having difficulties securing a firm grip with my thumb, which seemed to have lost most of its strength and dexterity. As time passed, I continued to experience a waking limb type sensation in my right hand and was forced to carry things with my left hand to avoid dropping them. Showing no signs of improvement, I scheduled an appointment with my primary care physician.

After looking over the injury, my doctor sent the following request to a specialized hand clinic: *I request consultation regarding diagnosis and/or treatment recommendation for persistent radial neuropathy of R hand at the wrist.* In the consultation request the doctor added the following notes: *Check hand and thumb injury from hand cuffing that occurred in mid-June. No improvement in dexterity or movement and has worsened since then. Patient has numbness and twitching of the thumb, as well as pain extending into other areas of the hand and forearm.* A couple weeks after the referral, I was admitted to the Dean Hand and Upper Extremity Clinic.

My first trip to the hand clinic resulted in an X-ray examination of my wrist along with a consultation with a doctor that specialized in hand and wrist surgery. The doctor informed me that while my wrists weren't broken, there appeared to be a substantial amount of nerve damage. Further tests were ordered and a week later I returned to the clinic for a battery of painful nerve tests. These tests included motor and sensory nerve tests where electrode patches were placed on my skin and the nerves were stimulated by electrical impulse.

My test results showed damage to the radial nerve along with carpal tunnel. I was fitted for a custom wrist brace and given two injections: one for carpal tunnel therapy and another for pain. Overall, I was told my wrist and damaged nerves should recover with time and rest. I was instructed to wear the wrist brace for a minimum of ninety days before returning for a recheck.

While my wrist eventually healed, my perception of the police was further marred. I was emotionally damaged by DK7 and other capitol police officers, but never was I physically hurt by an officer's intentional actions. Overall, I felt betrayed by an individual with power and the utmost authority.

Not only was I arrested in the most secure location, a police station, but I was also a completely compliant subject. In return for my cooperation, I was rewarded with brutality and indifference. The arresting/transporting officer blatantly disregarded his training to teach me a lesson.

If an officer could do this to a submissive subject without provocation, imagine the horrors he could inflict in a situation where he was directly disrespected or provoked.

Now, imagine what the same individual could be capable of when he felt threatened or could articulate "fear for his life."

It is a terrifying reality, and one that individuals throughout the US face daily. Comply and get hurt, disobey and you may die.

CHAPTER 19

DETOX IS MESSY

———

After being arrested, life began to change.

The title and job position I had worked years to secure dissolved overnight. The illusion of being okay, transformed into questions of "how bad is it" and "is there anything I/we can do to help."

Despite offers from immediate family to assist, I believed I had to confront the problem within myself first. After entering a mentally and physically addictive relationship with opioids two years prior, I needed to pursue the messiest breakup of my life. The time to detox from opioids had arrived.

It was late July 2012, and my wife, who acted more like a roommate, was away for the weekend. She took Bonsai with her, so Karma and I were holding down the fort. I began preparations to detox by making a trip to Walgreens for necessary essentials. There I purchased multiple bottles of Pedialyte, along with Gatorade, to aid with preventing dehydration. I also bought a bottle of Aleve, a box of protein bars, and a case of water. My thought process was to gather all the supplies in the master bathroom and spend most of the weekend traveling between the bed and the toilet.

I also factored Karma's needs into the situation.

I relocated her bag of dog food, along with her dishes and dog bed into the master bedroom. In case I was too weak, or physically unable to let her outside, I propped open the patio door leading to the fenced in backyard. Overall, I was more concerned about Karma's well-being than my own and wanted to ensure her basic needs were met throughout the weekend. Once everything was in place, I treated the two of us to a steak dinner, which served as a symbolic last meal. I was about to say goodbye to my old, addicted self.

After we ate, I held a conversation with Karma in the kitchen, as if I were talking to a friend. I promised her that "no matter how bad things got, I would pull through and be there for her." I also guaranteed that "for as long as I lived, she would have a loving home and someone to watch over her."

By promising these things to Karma, I was also making a pledge to myself; failure was not an option.

With that mentality in mind, I gathered the remainder of my pain medication, which was hidden in the false bottom of an Ajax container underneath the kitchen sink. Without thinking or hesitation, I dumped the pills into the garbage disposal and let the machine do its work. Now, there was no turning back.

The next forty-eight hours of withdrawal were among the most difficult days of my life. First, my anxiety spiked. I transitioned from being highly confident that I could complete the process, to convincing myself that I was going to die without another fix. Again, I was riding another one of life's roller coasters. As each minute passed, the temptation to give up and call Jon became almost intoxicating. I remember picking up my cell phone and beginning to text him, only to erase the text, and immediately restart the process.

As my cravings to consume a pill grew, I diverted my attention toward Karma. I must have petted her for an hour straight to self-soothe, while my thoughts spiraled out of control. The sheer anticipation of what detox symptom was to come next drove me temporarily insane. I could only fathom guesses as to what I was about to face. Without clarity, anxiety alone was about to consume me from the inside out, and then I began to vomit.

The nausea lasted for hours. Every movement I made brought upon a new wave of stomach pyrotechnics. After purging the steak dinner, along with the remainder of my stomach contents, I began throwing up bile.

The yellow fluid had a consistency of slime. I gagged on bile strands that extended down the back of my throat. All attempts to consume fluids to wash it down were dominated by the involuntary reflux to immediately throw up. Despite my best attempts to stay hydrated, I couldn't keep anything down for more than a few minutes. Water, Gatorade, Pedialyte, it made no difference as everything was immediately purged from my system. I remained locked in this vicious cycle throughout the night. All the while, Karma remained close, as if she were watching over me like a guardian sent from above.

The entire next day consisted of more of the same. Every attempt to move was matched by my body's desire to rid itself of the remaining toxins. This phase of detox came coupled with a state of delirium, and I began to confuse reality with fiction. My cognition became so distorted, that I believed I was watching myself decontaminate from a perspective outside of my own. I felt as if I were a fly on the wall witnessing my own undoing. Violent episodes of shaking kept me grounded, however, as they returned me to my frame.

My body was wracked by chills. I felt like I was burning up. Throughout the feverish dreams, I remember screaming for Karma, pleading for her to stay at my side. For hours, she remained the only thing that kept me grounded, as I laid semi-lucid on the bathroom floor. Without Karma's presence, I doubt I would have maintained the desire to see another day. When Sunday finally arrived, it came with the worst migraine one could imagine. My brain felt as though a carnivorous worm was tunneling through the layers of gray matter. Every nerve cell acted as if they were firing all at once, creating an electrical storm inside my head. The Aleve that I purchased offered little relief, and I laid curled around the toilet as the hours passed by.

At some point throughout the day, it began to rain. The thunder resonated to the beats inside my mind. Karma, who suffered from severe storm anxiety, sat partially on top of me seeking solace from the roaring sky. While the rain fell, I began to successfully consume water for the first time in two days.

After spending 48 hours mostly on the bathroom floor, my body was dehydrated and stiff with pain. I sporadically trembled and felt extremely weak, but my cognition slowly began to return. Karma and I gradually relocated from the bathroom to the family room couch. I was finally able to keep down the water, so I switched to Pedialyte to rehydrate, after spending the past two days purging.

Like the state Karma was in when I rescued her from the tree, I found myself alive, but far from recovered.

It took another handful of days before I began to feel myself, and even that felt unfamiliar. Like Karma and the repetitious leash training, I needed to retrain both my mind and body to function without the pills. To be successful, I knew I was not going to be able to complete such a massive undertaking alone. Again, I thought of how Karma initially needed me to survive; now, I needed someone else.

Later that evening, with my head still pounding, I began to research counseling and rehabilitation facilities in my area. After enduring the risky home detox, I was convinced that an outpatient facility would adequately fit my needs. Eventually, I settled upon Connections Counseling. I remember choosing Connections over all the other facilities because I liked the name. I also felt the need to reconnect to everything addiction had taken from me, and the namesake provided some hope of follow-through. Prior to passing out on the couch, I promised myself, along with Karma who was lying nearby, to call Connections in the morning.

I had taken the first step to recovery with my detox, but there was a longer road ahead.

CHAPTER 20

ROAD TO RECOVERY

Recovery from any substance abuse disorder is fucking hard. Experiencing success in recovery is even harder.

When I began receiving counseling services for opioid abuse, I treated the sessions with my counselor like a college course. I strived to obtain as much knowledge as I could about overcoming addiction, and then looked to apply the same principles to my life.

My counselor Shelly, who was flourishing in her own recovery, stated, "many individuals experienced higher levels of success in recovery when they pair counseling with an Alcoholics Anonymous (AA) or Narcotics Anonymous (NA) program." Like a student of recovery, I paired my weekly counseling sessions with a daily AA or NA meeting.

By surrounding myself with people in recovery, I immediately felt less unique. Hearing the testimonies of others made me feel like I was surrounded by likeminded individuals. Countless times throughout a meeting, someone would reveal what seemed to be an individual battle, only to have the event endorsed by other members with a shared recovery experience. For me, AA and NA meetings provided a safe space to share internal battles with cravings and the thoughts of using of which I was fighting.

These meetings proved even more pivotal after my wife opted out of our partnership.

Shortly after losing my Security Supervisor position with the UW Police Department, I began working as a server and part-time caterer for a local diner. One day after working a double shift at the restaurant, I came home to find my brother and best friend Josh at my house waiting in the driveway. This was unusual, since both lived over an hour away, and I was not expecting a visit from either of them. It wasn't until I opened the front door to a near empty living room that I realized what had occurred. While I was working, my wife, along with her family and a few friends, removed all her belongings from the house. My brother and Josh were there to support me in the aftermath.

Initially, I was shocked to see the house that empty, but not surprised by the overall act of her moving out. Our relationship was virtually nonexistent. We hadn't spoken for several weeks, nor were we sleeping in the same bedroom. She also demonstrated a complete disinterest in my recovery, while confiding to Josh that she believed, "I merely had a problem with caffeine and possibly alcohol."

Whether she simply didn't care, or I had hidden my opioid addiction from her so well that she truly didn't know, I cannot ascertain. However, I can confirm that she bailed in the moment that I needed someone most. Fortunately, she left the one thing I cared about the most: Karma.

Karma remained my reason for being sober throughout recovery, especially early on.

As I continued to struggle with cravings, or the overwhelming urge to use, I would take Karma for a long walk.

While we walked together, I used to verbally proclaim any indiscretions I was considering. For example, I shared how "driving on campus could be triggering, since I passed spots where I once used." I also explained what I was learning in counseling about recovery to Karma. Terms like "euphoric recall" and "cross addiction" were clarified as we covered miles of concrete sidewalks together. Anything I needed to share, I told to Karma. Eventually, I began trading trips to the gym for trips to the dog park. As the bond between Karma and me grew even stronger, I felt like I had a reason to continue fighting for a new life.

Eventually, I began substituting other unhealthy habits that kept me stuck in addiction for those that were new and uncomfortable. I exchanged gym dates with Jon for sober dates at home. I stopped isolating and opened my house to other individuals struggling with addiction. I even hosted sober events that were publicized during Connection Counseling group sessions. Oftentimes, Karma would become the highlight of such events.

She naturally gravitated toward the person who was sitting alone and begged for his/her attention. Karma's ability to break the ice with other individuals, especially those in the early stages of recovery where life seems unmanageable, was unmatched. She played the role of entertainer, while I sat back and got reacquainted with my sober self.

Despite the new lease on life that sobriety provided, I was still facing a massive legal case from the thefts I committed while in active addiction.

On October 29, 2012, I made an initial appearance in court on a total of fourteen misdemeanor counts of theft and false representation. Seeing that I was sober, working, and making additional strides toward overall recovery, the judge granted a signature bond of 500 dollars per count. This meant that I was able to sign and pay to remain in the community while my case progressed through the legal system.

Despite the recovery progress I was making, I was constantly thinking about sentencing and the high probability that I would eventually go to jail. When I wasn't battling an opioid craving, I was crippled with anxiety over what my future held.

As each pretrial conference date drew closer, my anxiety rose to the point where I would barely sleep or eat for days at a time. It wasn't that I didn't want to practice proper self-care, but more like I didn't feel worthy of receiving the basic human essentials.

I felt so ashamed of my past actions that I started believing I was the sum of my worst discretions.

As I tried to move forward with life, the burden of knowing that I stole from and negatively impacted others became a weight I could not bear. Thoughts of suicide began to preoccupy my mind. Although I didn't make an attempt to take my life in these moments of shame, I certainly believed the world would be a better place without me. As I sunk into a depressive low, months passed between court dates.

On January 16, 2013, a final pretrial conference was held. Neither my attorney nor the prosecuting district attorney (DA) could agree on a potential plea bargain deal. A joint request for a 45-day extension was filed. Next, a new final pre-trial date was scheduled toward the end of March.

While the court procedures sluggishly proceeded, I did everything in my power to occupy my mind and suppress intrusive thoughts. This included attending more AA and NA meetings, while staying sober and continuing counseling. I also worked a ridiculous number of hours serving at the restaurant and catering events on the weekends. Despite experiencing sporadic back pain and spasms, especially after long catering events, I learned to work through the agony without taking a pill.

Slowly, I began the process of retraining my body to acknowledge pain without becoming overwhelmed by its presence. The motto, "pain is only temporary" is something I would repeat to myself countless times throughout a long day or difficult shift. When the pain became too overwhelming, I turned to ice and rest, as opposed to trying to push through it like I did in the past. Effectively managing my back pain allowed me to work both jobs without experiencing any major physical setbacks.

Despite the physically exhausting nature of the work, I continued to work both positions for several months. By doing both, I was also able to scrape together enough money each month to cover my mortgage payments. My mom also helped supplement my income by providing a monthly check to assist in paying for other essentials like electricity, water, and groceries. Her financial aid kept me from receiving past due notices as I toiled to ensure my basic needs were satisfied.

Despite my mother's support, money remained incredibly tight. I frequently depended on my starting server bank of ten dollars to put enough gas in my car to make it to work. Once at work, I relied on my serving skills and subsequent tips to replenish the starting bank. Each day, I repeated this process, while saving everything over the ten-dollar opening bank amount. Every additional cent I made went toward paying my mortgage or legal fees. Operating with my fuel tank on empty became the norm. Like my car, I was running on fumes, but still ultimately making it to where I needed to be.

This manner of survival repeated itself until May 10, 2013, when I agreed to a plea deal.

CHAPTER 21

LOCKED UP

———

Shortly after agreeing to the plea deal on May 10, I began serving time in Dane County Jail.

My lawyer and the district attorney agreed upon the following terms. From the date of the plea bargain, I was allotted thirteen days to "get my affairs in order," prior to reporting to jail. Next, I would serve ninety days within the county jail. After completing three months jail time, I would be placed on misdemeanor probation for three years. As I waited to be incarcerated, I was an anxious mess. Overall, there were three major factors driving my anxiety. The first was Karma.

Prior to going to jail, I had never spent more than an evening or two away from Karma. I feared that in my absence, she would suffer, especially from separation anxiety. Since I knew I would struggle immensely being away from Karma, I could only imagine the unease she would feel while I was away. I feared she would think I abandoned her, and I had no way to convey otherwise.

I also worried that she wouldn't respond well to my mom or brother, who would be serving as her interim caregivers. Despite the additional training she had received at dog day camp, I had no idea how she would react to being cared for by someone that wasn't me. This kept me up most nights.

Ultimately, Karma was the last piece of a broken life that I cared for, and I certainly did not want to see her progression negatively impacted by my time away. Even more than I hated the thought of going to jail, I hated knowing that I would not be there for Karma. Aside from Karma, I was concerned about my finances, primarily my mortgage.

As I previously mentioned, money was incredibly tight. I was working sixty plus hour weeks to survive, and even that was barely enough. There wasn't a chance in hell I was going to afford three months of mortgage payments while I was in jail. Fortunately, my mother offered to liquidate some of her long-term investments to keep me from falling behind on mortgage payments.

In addition, her brother, who also worked as an AODA counselor and understood my affliction, agreed to help support me by covering 7,500 dollars of my legal fees. In a letter to my attorney, he wrote, "I consider Travis a surrogate son and I want him to weather this storm and successfully move forward with his life." Without his support at the time, I certainly would not be here writing a memoir today. Once I had the financial piece of going to jail covered, I still had one last major concern. What if another inmate recognized me?

When I was booked into Dane County Jail on May 23, 2013, I had little idea of what to expect. Of all the undergraduate courses I took as a Criminal Justice major, not even one offered any clarity on how to survive serving time as a former officer. What I recalled learning about jail was also extremely troubling. From my studies, I remembered that jail time was considered the hardest time to serve. This was because jail time, unlike prison time, is designed to be short-term.

This means that jails frequently have less structured programs than prisons.

As a person that suffers from anxiety, continual change coupled with little daily routine, created a situation where I was in constant distress. Essentially, jail time became time served in a perpetual state of adjustment. Since adjustment or change is difficult, time in jail was also exceedingly difficult.

Furthermore, county jails typically house those awaiting trial, along with those serving misdemeanor sentences. People awaiting trial for brutal crimes were mixed in with others who had unpaid child support. This made for a revolving door type situation within the jail, where individuals of all types were constantly rotated in and out. Some would serve a weekend, where others would serve months while awaiting trial.

The next thing I noticed about Dane County Jail was its inmates were disproportionately black. Historically, Dane County Jail is comprised of 40 percent African American inmates, whereas, according to the 2019 US Census Data, African Americans only make up 5.5 percent of the county's population (US Census Bureau). Furthermore, the Hispanic population within the jail also seemed extremely over-represented compared to the 6.5 percent of the population they comprise in Dane County (US Census Bureau).

Overall, I found myself in a sea of black and brown faces that didn't match the greater community from where I came. This was the first instance in my life where I was the minority in the population.

However, unlike what is shown on television, divisions within population groups in Dane County Jail had little to do with race. Instead, individuals typically grouped together based on how they opted to spend their free time. "Gamblers" made up one of the largest groups within the jail population. With little to do, many inmates would utilize their canteen, or commissary purchased weekly, as betting collateral. Bets were placed on the widest variety of things ranging from which deputy would work the next shift, to sporting events, card games, and dominoes. From what I observed, the fastest way for an inmate to get into an altercation was to place a bet and be unable to cover if they lost.

I avoided the gambling spectacle by only purchasing essential items through commissary, like deodorant, bar soap, and toothpaste. By not having anything to gamble with, I could easily dodge encounters where other inmates would ask if I wanted to "buy in." Avoiding confrontation in jail was my primary means of survival. I simply wanted to serve my time and survive so I could be reunited with Karma. Another method I utilized to stay safe was reading.

For some reason I recalled the song "Son of a Sailor" by Jimmy Buffett. I always found the line about reading books about heroes and crooks to be inspiring and I took refuge in that idea.

While locked up, I read everything I could get my hands on. Not only did it help to pass the time, but I was able to escape my own thoughts and feelings for a while. Whenever I felt my anxiety peaking, I would retreat to my bunk and read whatever novel I had selected off the jail library book cart. While I never enjoyed reading as a child, within the confines of concrete and steel, reading became my favorite pastime. When I wasn't reading, I doodled.

As the son of an art teacher, I spent much of my middle school life perfecting my doodling skills. While in jail, these skills were desired by other inmates who wanted to personalize letters home or to show love to a significant other/ child. Others wanted tattoo designs to be inked once they got out. Regardless of the request, I quickly discovered that I could trade my drawing ability for commissary items.

Through the act of trade, I was able to eliminate my weekly canteen costs while continuing to avoid the gambling scene. It was a win/win situation for me, as drawing for others became my calling within the jail pod. Soon, inmates identified me as the pod artist, and I worried less about being viewed as a cop. Each drawing I did for another inmate also helped to pass the time.

Aside from reading and illustrating, the other way I survived 90 days in jail was limiting my calls home.

It may seem counterintuitive, but constantly calling home from jail serves as a trap for many inmates.

While everyone inside wants to know and be a part of what's occurring on the outside, they have no means of control over the outside world. Therefore, many individuals that spend ample amounts of time on the phone tend to get caught up and fixated upon situations outside of jail they cannot change. These situations tend to slowly eat away at the inmate, while highlighting the difference between freedom and incarceration.

Instead of calling home daily, I would limit my calls to 2-3 per week. Not only did this help keep the costs of being in jail down, but also allowed me to "check in" without becoming obsessed with what I was missing on the outside. Limiting jail phone time also aided in my emotional regulation overall.

If I called home and asked about Karma, I would often get off the phone extremely depressed, despite hearing that she was doing well. By limiting the number of calls I was making out, I was able to stay emotionally neutral, or at least appear that way in front of the other inmates. Keeping my feelings in check helped make the time I was serving less intrusive.

Ultimately, each inmate discovers what helps them serve the time they owe. What worked for me the first time in jail may not work for another individual. Additionally, had another inmate discovered that I was a former officer, my time spent in Dane County Jail would have been completely different. Because I was able to conceal my past identity and adapt to my surrounding environment, I was able to survive.

However, 3 months of lying, coupled with heightened anxiety certainly took its toll on my overall mental health. I entered jail confident in my ability to stay sober, but several weeks without counseling and my support system left me feeling vulnerable and alone. Despite serving my time, I was released from Dane County Jail in a far worse mental state from which I had entered. Soon, it would be revealed just how far I had fallen.

CHAPTER 22

ROCK BOTTOM

After returning home from Dane County Jail, life became more difficult. Within 24 hours of my release, I was required to report to the Dane County Probation and Parole office. After meeting with my assigned agent and receiving the rules of probation, I begrudgingly began serving an additional 3 years on paper. The phrase "on paper" is slang, or the street way of saying that someone is on probation and is commonly used by individuals who have been incarcerated.

For me, being on paper meant that I remained trapped within the criminal justice system. One misstep and I would immediately be sent back to jail. To make matters worse, I was required to inform potential employers that I was on probation. This made the prospect of obtaining a job with a competitive wage nearly impossible. Essentially, I had to take whatever work I could get. With my savings wiped out by legal fees and the mortgage due, I needed to start making money as quickly as possible. My mom helped while I was in jail, but I felt guilty continually taking her handouts. I wanted to fully support myself.

Fortunately, the diner where I was previously serving and catering agreed to hire me back. This alleviated some of the immense financial strain I was under; however, it did not provide room for anything aside from absolute essentials.

In addition, Karma was returned to me from my mother's care. She arrived home slightly overweight after being completely spoiled while I was away. I still remember her shaking uncontrollably, while jumping in a circular motion, when my brother brought her through the front door. She was more excited than I ever saw her, and I immediately burst into tears. Three months without my best friend left me tired and defeated but having her home, happy and healthy, brought some life back into me. It became my goal to ride the positive wave of emotion for as long as possible.

Just as life seemed to be sorting itself out, I found myself in a new battle with my mental health. It was another typical high/low situation. As I found myself on what looked to be an upward trend, I encountered another devastating low.

On October 10, 2013, I hit rock bottom.

I was at the pinnacle of a month-long manic episode, or phase of bipolar depression in which hyperactivity and sleepless nights ruled my existence. After going two, possibly three days without sleep, my cognition was an absolute mess. For the sake of my sanity, I became desperate for sleep. While seeking serenity, I took a Trazodone, a tool prescribed to me to help combat insomnia.

On that particular evening, however, sleep continued to evade me. After lying in bed for what seemed like hours, I opted to head downstairs into the kitchen to pour myself a stiff drink. Although having/consuming alcohol was a violation of my probation, I learned combining alcohol with the Trazodone was a surefire way to obtain the sleep I desperately needed while on a manic high.

I recall thinking to myself that this concoction will assure I pass out and get some sleep tonight. I could not have been more wrong.

After re-watching SportsCenter for the second, possibly third time, I took to the garage to continue a furniture restoration project I began months prior. This conduct was also common in times of mania, as I would creatively dive into any transitory fix that sparked my interest in the moment. After about an hour of wood staining, I was still wide awake and seeking more exhilarating escapades from the expiring evening. A few text messages later, I found myself behind the wheel and headed to a local bar exactly one mile from my home.

I arrived at the bar just before midnight. This allotted two hours of heavy consumption before the bartender would announce "last call." Ample time to get intoxicated before heading back home to pass out.

Drinking for effect over taste, I ordered a long island with light ice and a splash of cola.

As I drank, I conversed intermittently with Thursday night regulars and found some comfort in engaging in conversation outside of my incessant thoughts. Stories of bar league softball filled the room, as I temporarily forgot my troubles. Unlike the time I had just spent lying restlessly awake in bed, the time at the bar passed quickly. Before I knew it, I had finished my sixth long island and was headed home. The short drive posed little risk of being pulled over, so I took my chances behind the wheel.

Just as I took the final left turn into my neighborhood, I over-accelerated and caused my car to go careening into the curb. The front right tire, along with the lower portion of the front clip, absorbed much of the impact as plastic pieces cracked under the pressure. Less than two blocks from home, I attempted to drive the car off the curb, but something was binding the tire to the damaged wheel well.

At that moment, I began to feel nauseated, and abandoned the damaged vehicle in search of a place to vomit. After a brief scan, I picked a secluded spot on the neighbor's side yard to throw up.

After vomiting and urinating on my neighbor's bushes, I struggled to collect myself for the short walk home. As I ventured from the cover of darkness, I felt another wave of nausea rush over me. Leaning against a parked vehicle in the driveway, I vomited again.

Only this time, I was using the vehicle's door handle as an aid to keep me upright, and I set off the car alarm.

In an instant, the blaring horn alerted those who had been sleeping to my presence. The front lights of a nearby porch flicked on, and I was reeling for a place to hide.

Too intoxicated to run, I stumbled to the adjacent neighbor's driveway and tried concealing myself behind another parked vehicle.

However, I quickly realized my six foot, two hundred plus pound frame was exposed. As the shrieking car horn was silenced, I could hear a man's voice screaming obscenities in the distance. Like a scared child, I slid into the front driver's seat of the unlocked vehicle and attempted to hide.

When the infuriated neighbor approached the vehicle, I initially refused to open the door. Instead, I attempted to reason with the irate individual through the closed window in hopes he would believe my story and leave me be. Momentarily, he stopped yelling and seemed receptive to hearing what I had to say, so I exited the vehicle. In my inebriated state, I stumbled while exiting the car and struggled to regain my balance.

According to the police report, the neighbor felt "threatened by the sudden movement" and "in that instant, went into defense mode." While on route, police dispatch advised that the caller's husband had "chased after the suspect and was currently striking him with a flashlight." While I thought the situation was under control, all it took was a stumble to throw me right back into the chaos.

Acting as the primary aggressor, the neighbor utilized a heavy-duty Maglite flashlight to "hit me as hard as he could." Instantaneously, my skull fractured like a coconut being struck by a hammer.

I cried out, "I didn't do anything;" as another devastating blow was dealt.

This strike caused me to temporarily lose consciousness, and I collapsed on the cement driveway.

Still unsatisfied with the damage he inflicted, the neighbor dealt a finishing blow to the back of my head as I laid unconscious. All I remember is a shockwave of the most intense pain I have ever felt, followed by absolute darkness.

When I regained consciousness, the police had arrived on the scene. They diligently amassed victim statements, making sure to articulate that the neighbor "felt fear for his safety" prior to unleashing an onslaught of blows.

Furthermore, they collected the two staining paint brushes from my jacket and entered them in as evidence. According to one officer's report, the brushes could be used to wipe away latent fingerprints, thus qualify them as burglary tools.

While the officers continued collecting statements, EMS arrived on the scene and assessed the situation. They took one look at my injuries and dispatched me to the closest hospital as quickly as possible.

Within hours, I would discover how one man's rage coupled with a solid flashlight would forever change my life and leave me permanently disabled.

CHAPTER 23

KARMA

I went to the hospital and Karma went back to live with my mom. If only things had been that simple.

Initially, I was taken to St. Mary's Hospital and immediately attended to by an emergency room nurse and doctor. The attending doctor informed the police officer that was standing by that I had "suffered significant facial fractures, that were in need of surgery."

A few hours into my stay at St. Mary's Hospital, it was determined that my injuries were even more extensive than the doctor originally thought. Since the neighboring UW Hospital was better equipped to deal with my head injury, possible brain trauma, and the impending surgery, I was transferred into their care.

Prior to being transported, it was determined by a Madison Police Sgt. that I would be arrested for disorderly conduct and attempted theft. Misdemeanor citations were issued for both offenses and my probation officer was to be notified of the violations later that day.

All the events I have just described to you, I do not remember. Instead, the incidents have been pieced together by combing through police reports. To date, I have no recollection of ever being at St. Mary's Hospital. However, I am extremely grateful for the care they provided and that I was promptly transferred to UW Hospital once they discovered the extent of my injuries.

The first thing I recall is being told by a nurse at UW Hospital that I would be meeting with a surgeon to discuss concerns about air reaching my brain cavity. While I was reviewing surgery options, the Madison Police were having a discussion of their own.

On October 10, 2013, at 6:44 a.m., a Madison Detective sent an email to an Assistant District Attorney stating the following: "attached are our briefing notes from last night. I will look into it when I get in. Apparently, he (Sackett) has a hard time learning the #1 rule of probation is not to commit further crime. What a moron."

While the assistant DA did not respond, another officer wrote, "Good grief. What a moron. He'll end up in prison yet, which is what he deserves."

Finally, a third officer chimed in and stated, "Oh my!!! Can you spell revocation!!!!!! He is out of control. I bet he is responsible for half of the east district crimes. Just put a GPS chip in him and be done with patrol work!"

While the officers made assumptions about my criminality, nobody thought to check the recent police reports from my neighborhood.

Had any one of the officers been focused on doing their job, instead of spouting insults and accusations, they would have realized that my vehicle was broken into a few weeks prior on September 25, 2013. At that time, our neighborhood was experiencing a high volume of vehicle break-ins and my car was no exception. I filed a police report under case number 13-302186 in which it is documented that I had my wallet stolen along with thirty-one dollars, black Oakley sunglasses, and a special wood grain pen I received while in college. My wallet was eventually recovered, but the money inside was missing.

I felt it necessary to include this in my story because it shows the power of the criminal label. Once I was labeled a criminal and on probation, it was immediately assumed that I was guilty of committing multiple other crimes despite the facts stating otherwise. The police were looking for a scapegoat and I provided them one the evening my head was smashed in. Speaking of which, I should also explain the magnitude of my injuries.

First, I suffered a traumatic brain injury, also known as a TBI.

One top of the TBI, I had fractures involving the left orbital wall, roof, and possibly nasolacrimal duct. A CT scan of my head also revealed non-displaced bilateral nasal bone fractures, along with a non-displaced fracture of the anterior process of the right maxilla. Finally, I was diagnosed with pneumocephalus or the presence of air within the cranial cavity, coupled with a cerebral contusion.

Following the evaluation in the emergency department by neurosurgery and ophthalmology, Trauma Service was consulted for admission. At that time, I was found to have no life-threatening injuries; however, trauma surgery was required to correct the orbital fractures along with the pneumocephalus. Three titanium plates were utilized to secure the fractures and air within my cranial cavity was expelled.

The next morning, on October 11, 2013, I had an additional surgery to repair the roof of my mouth. Upon the conclusion of that surgery, I returned to the emergency unit and begin the long process of recovery.

Initially, I thought I would be in the hospital for a minimum of four days since I had a follow up ophthalmology appointment on October 15, 2013. I vaguely remember snapshots from this period, comprised of fragments of memories made while lying in a hospital bed. Despite my best efforts to recall what I was feeling, all I can truly remember is the pain. The pain of having your skull broken in multiple places is unlike any other pain I have ever felt. It was so intense that even writing about it today makes me feel nauseous. In fact, I have already had to take multiple breaks from composing, simply to complete this chapter.

The amount of pain I was in post-surgery, even with administered narcotics, was unfathomable.

As an individual that tolerates pain relatively well, I would not wish that level of discomfort on my worst enemy. Reflecting upon the unbearable pain, the only component that rivaled the physical discomfort was mentally trying to cope with my actions.

As I laid in the hospital recovery bed, I felt two primary emotions: shame and guilt. The shame stemmed from relapsing. Not only did I let myself down, but I also let those down who had shown me support during my initial nosedive. Furthermore, I felt guilty that I wasn't able to overcome my vices the first time around and truly master recovery. At the time, I had not been diagnosed with bipolar disorder. Since I didn't know the extent of my mental illness, I continued to blame myself.

Eventually, I would learn that I put a Band-Aid on a much larger "wound" and expected it to hold.

In that hospital bed, I discovered that to fully recover, I was going to need additional mental health treatment. It was an impossibly hard way to learn a lesson.

Fleeting moments of mental clarity are all I have from the next two days following surgery. I recall thinking of Karma and questioning how much time I was going to spend apart from her. I was also furious with myself for jeopardizing our future together. She deserved more consistency, and I continued to let her down. Did I even warrant her continued love and companionship?

As I struggled to regain some perspective on life moving forward, I was hit with another devastating blow.

On October 13, 2013, not even two days removed from my second surgery, I was taken from UW Hospital and brought back to Dane County Jail.

CHAPTER 24

TBI RECOVERY IN JAIL

Whoever made the decision to have me recover from multiple surgeries in Dane County Jail is an absolute monster!

In less than 72 hours, I relapsed, nearly got beaten to death, suffered a TBI, had two surgeries to repair my extensive injuries, and was now expected to recover inside the jail walls.

When I was brought to Dane County Jail, I immediately expressed concerns for my overall safety. I hadn't left a hospital bed in almost three days. Earlier that morning, the hospital nursing staff set a goal of using the bathroom by myself; now I was expected to cope and recover in jail.

To make matters worse, my left eye was swollen completely shut. I had limited vision and depth perception which made fending for myself nearly impossible. During the booking process, I expressed all these apprehensions to an intake worker who documented them into progress notes. I relied on the same progress notes to explain what transpired after I was booked into Dane County Jail. Without them, this period would remain one painful blur.

Since Dane County Jail had no medical unit, it was decided that I would be placed in segregation, which also doubles as Dane County Jail's solitary confinement. According to the progress note, I was "placed in seg, given an xtra bed roll, instructed not to blow [my] nose, protect [my] head, and given 2 Percocets and 1 Zofran. It was also ordered that I have my vitals checked twice per shift with neuros."

Concluding the intake process, I was brought to segregation and placed in a small concrete cell. Inside my cell was a raised concrete slab where I could place my bed roll, a combination sink and toilet, and a surveillance camera mounted in the ceiling. There were no additional amenities.

Unlike the hospital, I did not have any way to access immediate medical attention.

Instead, I was instructed to pound on the cell door and shout for a guard should an emergency medical situation occur. The progress note from my first day in segregation read "keep I/M (inmate) in seg for close monitoring and safety. Check vitals and neuro exam every 4 hours. Follow up with trauma surgery as scheduled."

On October 15, 2013, I was brought back to UW Hospital for an ophthalmology appointment. The evaluation was for the left orbital fracture I had sustained. I was escorted by two Dane County Sheriff deputies and felt completely dejected being paraded through the hospital with my law enforcement handlers. As the deputies searched for the ophthalmology department, hospital patients stared at me. Parents shielded their children as I shuffled by in shackles.

Seeing parents block their children from the mere sight of me left me completely broken inside. In those moments, I was viewed as the bad guy. Once responsible for the safety of the governor, I was reduced to a potential threat that could keep kids awake at night. Whereas I once longed for Hulk Hogan to save me as a child, I was now the villain from which others needed protection. By the time we reached ophthalmology, I was questioning my role in society.

The rest of the appointment, which I've transcribed from UW Health patient notes goes as follows: "He has done well following surgery. Swelling is improving. Pain is still 7-8/10, using 2 Percocet every 4 hours. He is sensitive to light and sound. He does not notice any diplopia (double vision). He does notice worms squiggling through his vision from time to time."

Although I do not remember, I must have also mentioned to the Ophthalmologist that I was constipated, because they included a recommendation for a stool softener. After the appointment, I was immediately brought back to Dane County Jail.

Little did I know, but that appointment would be the only follow up to surgery that I would receive.

Once back inside the jail, I began to break down mentally. I was placed on a self-harm and mental health watch. The watch was initiated by the jail's mental health staff. Although I do not recall the events leading to the watch, a member of mental health wrote the following description:

> "I/M depressed about current situation, stated that he does not remember much of what happened. I/M was placed in seg due to fear of being harmed by others—appearance and medical issues. I/M had lengthy pause before answering safety questions. He then said that he does fear for his safety—initially by others but then said that he is not sure he feels safe with himself. I/M stated that the 'only way he would probably do something (hurt himself) would be to get to the hospital and out of jail.'"

These words are extremely telling regarding my thoughts at the time. All I wanted was to leave jail and recover someplace I felt safe and protected. That day would not come anytime soon.

I spent two more days recovering in segregation. On October 16, 2013, it was reported that "I/M still wants to stay in seg as he is in a lot of physical pain and still cannot see out of his eye and does not feel safe to be around other inmates. No thoughts of suicide or self-harm."

Although recovering in segregation was horrible, I did not have to worry about my overall safety. The trade-off of staying in solitary confinement was worth the feeling of being safe inside the jail.

The next day, jail medical updated my vital checks to occur once per 24-hour shift. After that, they were to be discontinued completely if no issues arose. According to the mental health progress notes on October 17, 2013, "I/M presented engaged and stable. No safety concerns currently. Issues addressed."

However, later that day the mental health staff transcribed that "I/M stated he is doing better but still having emotions that do not reflect the state he is in. I/M stated the medical doctor explained this is normal with head injuries. I/M endorsed coping okay."

From what I am able to recall of those two days, my emotions were far from stable. One moment I felt like I could survive general population, the next, I was crippled with fear. Each emotion came and went without warning. I felt completely disconnected from my ability to control my feelings, and subsequently out of control in general.

Somewhere in those moments, I realized I lost everything. To recover from my injuries, especially in Dane County Jail,

I needed more support than what was being offered. In order to survive, I needed every ounce of strength I possessed.

The days to come would be hell. I had finally hit rock bottom.

CHAPTER 25

JAILHOUSE PT

———

On October 18, 2013, I was moved from segregation into general population.

Five days passed since I suffered the traumatic brain injury, and vision in my left eye was slowly returning. I continued to battle a lingering migraine, likely from the brain contusion, and was thoroughly struggling to grasp reality. Overall, I did not trust my surroundings, nor did I trust myself to successfully navigate through the complexities of jail pod existence.

On October 22, 2013, I submitted the following mental health request:

"I am having irrational thoughts/feelings that I fear are related to my recent head trauma. For example, on Monday Oct. 21st, I believed I had a research paper due for school. I felt panicked because I could not complete the assignment in jail. I have not been in school since for six years."

I completed a mental health assessment and was advised to do the following: "Use coping skills to deal with panic feelings and memory issues. I/M (inmate) has anxiety reduction techniques." Essentially, I was supposed to apply the coping skills I learned while undergoing AODA counseling to manage the complications of dealing with a TBI.

While most individuals with similar extensive injuries would be attending physical or occupational therapy, I was in jail serving as my own PT.

Two days later and still struggling, I tendered the following inmate medical request:

> "The headaches associated with my head injury are becoming more frequent and intense. I also feel that my sensitivity to sound has increased. Loud noises create a "shockwave" type sensation that seems to reverberate through my head. Finally, a fair amount of dried blood came out of my left ear prior to dinner. Overall, I do not feel well and am sleeping approximately 18 hours per day."

The jail responded by having me seen by medical four days later.

At that time, my left ear was checked and found to have no active bleeding. Headaches and aphasia, or the loss of ability to comprehend or express speech caused by brain damage, were also discussed. Ultimately, it was decided that I would be given Tylenol three times daily to help combat the headaches. Nothing was done for my aphasia, which was causing me to get stuck on common words while talking.

I continued to struggle while attempting to recover with limited jail resources. This prompted me to advocate for myself by submitting an additional medical request on October 25, 2013.

The request read as follows:

"Can I please receive a copy of any "aftercare" information provided by the hospital post-surgery? I was told I would be sent home with this information and never received anything once I got to jail. I would like to know if there is something that I can be doing to aid the recovery process according to the hospital aftercare information which has been withheld."

The medical staff responded by providing instructions on how to obtain copies of my medical records while in jail. These records were not entirely helpful at the time; however, they have proven pivotal in documenting my initial struggles post-TBI.

Without a clear pathway on how to approach recovery, fear and anxiety continued to rule my life.

On October 28, 2013, I submitted another mental health request. My chief complaint read:

"I am struggling with fear/anxiety related to my head injury. At times I feel "normal" but often stumble over words or simply forget what I'm saying or doing. I fear things are not improving or are even going to get worse. The mental health staff responded by writing, "Try not to push the panic button. This is still a recent head injury— just remember what your MD said—it takes time.""

I was tired of advocating for myself. It was clear the jail had no vested interest in my recovery, nor were they going to provide additional resources to assist me in recovering independently. Over the next month, I practiced my own version of occupational therapy.

To combat the aphasia, I started reading books aloud to myself. The repetition and process of completing sentences verbally seemed to aid in words flowing naturally during conversation. When I did get stuck on a word, I would picture it in my head and do my best to sound it out. The approach was remarkably similar to how I learned to read as a young child, yet it seemed to work well.

I also committed ample time to drawing and tracing letters. The more I re-familiarized myself with the shape each letter made, the easier it was to write out when I needed to submit a request. Despite having no guidance in how to properly recover from a TBI, I did my best to identify the areas I was struggling with and address them accordingly.

Regardless of my best efforts, my mental health remained unstable, and cognitive healing remained in question.

Amid recovery, I was served official divorce papers in jail. Although I knew the papers were eventually coming, the overall timing couldn't have been worse. I felt like I was hitting rock bottom repeatedly.

The hearing was scheduled for early December, and I was forced to attend in full jail uniform. Like the hospital appointment, I was fully shackled prior to standing before the judge. While I was not overly concerned about the divorce proceedings, I did not like appearing in front of others handcuffed with chains adjoining my hands and feet. It made me look and feel like a monster.

Each time I was placed in full restraints, I endured by thinking of Karma. If she was able to survive being chained to a tree, I could survive being restrained and dishonored.

Although I don't recall much from the divorce hearing, I do remember reflecting upon Karma. Her struggles made her strong, and mine could do the same for me. Just as I learned to do growing up in an abusive home, I found the grit to survive. Yet survival, continued to be a difficult task.

A few days following the divorce trial, I submitted a mental health request, my first in over a month. The request read:

> "I'm struggling to sleep/stay asleep at night. When I sleep, I frequently wake up in sweats and have nightmares. Most of the nightmares involve me getting beaten or severely hurt in some manner. I also find that I'm more anxious and "jumpy" while awake."

In response, the jail issued a 54-page PTSD, or post-traumatic stress disorder, workbook. This was the first piece of help literature I received from jail, and I was almost two months into my stay.

The patient treatment manual, which I still have today, was something that I worked through independently to help relieve some of the symptoms associated with PTSD. While it was not nearly as effective as one on one counseling, the workbook provided some additional structure to my self-made recovery program. Cautiously, I began interacting more with the other inmates in my unit.

From mid-December until the end of January when I was released, I survived by building a friendship. Cesar, who remains one of the largest males I have ever encountered, became my bunkmate while I was struggling to keep things together.

Despite his intimidating size, Cesar was a peaceful individual simply looking to serve out his time. With the common goal of wanting to leave Dane County Jail as soon as possible, Cesar and I avoided drama associated with gambling and other restricted jail activities. For Cesar, this meant spending a majority of his days working in the kitchen or translating Spanish to English for other inmates. For me, I passed the time working through the PTSD workbook and continued to practice tracing letters. When either of us needed a break, we made time for a game of cards and to talk about things to come.

Then one evening in late December, I woke up in the middle of the night and left my bunk. From there, I proceeded to sit on the bunk row floor and rock back and forward. Whether it was a side effect of the head injury, or a night terror I could not escape, my mind had me believing I was the passenger on a boat. Cesar woke up to me non-responsively swaying on the floor, and immediately alerted the guard to my situation when he could not "snap me out of it."

Mercifully, he took time to explain to the guard that I had recently suffered a head injury, or the unfamiliar guard could have easily responded to my noncompliance with force. Instead, Cesar and the guard worked together to get me situated at a table until jail medical staff arrived. After checking my vitals and providing some water, the medical staff cleared me to return to the pod. Later that morning after breakfast, Cesar recapped the night's events. I had absolutely no recollection of getting out of bed, let alone interacting with a guard. I was terrified, but ultimately unharmed.

Today, I attribute some of my survival to Cesar and his ability to show compassion toward an individual in need. While his actions may seem insignificant, he effectively spoke on my behalf when I could not speak for myself. In that moment, along with many others, he acted as the friend I desperately needed. In a chapter that has been difficult to articulate because I was unaided and struggled so severely, I want to conclude it by showing thanks.

With the help of an unexpected friend, I survived the most difficult segment of my battered life.

CHAPTER 26

REBUILDING WITH LIMITATIONS

——

After being released from Dane County Jail in January 2014, I owed the system more time.

Because my probation was revoked, I was accountable for an additional nine months of jail time to the county. Fortunately, Dane County has a Jail Diversion Program, where an inmate can live at home while serving his/her sentence.

The program is based on an electronic monitoring system where the inmate must always wear an ankle bracelet. Furthermore, the inmate can participate in Huber privileges, or the right to leave home for the purposes of work up to 8 hours per day. Some additional privileges are also permitted such as attending school (classes), going to alcohol or drug counseling, and up to one hour of grocery shopping per week if an inmate lives alone. Overall, the Jail Diversion Program is an opportunity for inmates to contribute to society while serving a sentence that would otherwise have them behind bars.

The first thing I did once I was released to the Jail Diversion Program was call my mother to have her bring Karma home. Life without Karma was lonely and depressing. To survive the next nine months on electronic monitoring, I needed Karma's company and unconditional love.

Having spent the past three months in jail recovering from the TBI, I was suffering from post-traumatic stress disorder (PTSD) and unprecedented levels of anxiety. I hoped that spending time with Karma would assist in calming my nerves and help restore me to a functioning baseline. Moreover, having her around would give me something to care for outside of myself and keep me focused on moving forward. In addition to adding Karma back into my life, I had to address the relapse which created the issue in the first place. To properly do that, I needed to return to Connections Counseling.

On February 1, 2014, I filled out a scholarship application for admittance into Connections Counseling intensive outpatient program (IOP). IO programs are for individuals who want or need a very structured recovery program with the flexibility to live at home and continue select responsibilities such as school or work. For this reason, the IO program paired perfectly with the Jail Diversion Program. Connections IOP consisted of three hours of treatment, three days per week in the mornings.

Once I was accepted into the program, I spent my mornings discussing the topics of addiction education, relapse prevention, and social support. Guest speakers also attended our sessions, and I was able to gain an immeasurable amount of insight into addiction from their shared experiences. The greatest takeaway from the speaker series was the consistent need to connect with other sober individuals in order to strengthen and protect one's own sobriety. While the past few months in jail did nothing to support my sobriety and left me feeling vulnerable to another relapse, the next twelve weeks in the Connections Counseling IO program focused on support and helped me address the root causes of my addictions.

After experiencing success with Connections IOP, I decided to stay on as a mentor and explore becoming an AODA counselor full-time. Multiple counselors at Connections struggled with addiction prior to finding their calling and this inspired me to seek a similar path. However, to make that dream a reality, I needed to overcome several obstacles.

The first obstacle I faced was purely medical. After suffering the TBI, I began experiencing migraines at an unprecedented rate. Vertigo, or the overwhelming sensation of loss of balance, commonly accompanied my migraines.

During a migraine, I suffer from severe pain on one side of my head, coupled with nausea and vomiting. These typically last 8 to 12 hours, with the most serious lasting over a day. If I attempt to push through the pain, I experience vertigo along with the other debilitating symptoms. Migraines became such a disruptive force in my life that my primary care doctor referred me to a neurologist.

After a battery of tests and multiple visits, a neuropsychology specialist diagnosed my condition as multifactorial cognitive dysfunction and chronic migraines without aura. Simply put, the migraines I experienced did not involve much light sensitivity.

Neither condition was present prior to the TBI; both were devitalizing in their own way.

Birthed in the aftermath of physical trauma, each diagnosis required a new normal to be established. For me, this meant learning to live outside of jail with a brain that no longer functioned as it once did. Despite these limiting factors, I continued to pursue becoming an AODA counselor.

The first week of April, I applied for and received student loan assistance for graduate school. I also began researching community counseling focused graduate programs. Eventually, I found one in my area that could potentially work in conjunction with the Jail Diversion program.

Lakeland College, where I completed my bachelor's degree, had a satellite campus in Madison that provided a counseling based graduate program. On top of that, Lakeland offered a summer semester, so if I were accepted, I could begin as early as late May. Even if I were admitted into the program, I had no idea if I would be able to handle the workload with my TBI, but I was certainly willing to try. Mid-April, I applied to the Community Counseling Graduate program at Lakeland College.

As I waited to hear back from graduate school, I continued doing improvements around the house.

I launched Operation Curb Appeal, where I installed hardscape beds in the front of the house and along the side yard. On top of these beds, I added select shrubs, along with a paver patio off the back deck with a nice fire pit. I kept costs low by doing all the labor myself and purchasing the materials just above cost from an upstart landscaping company. The manual labor was strenuous and caused notable discomfort in my lower back, but I did not let that deter me from my overall objective.

My goal was to enhance the value of the house while I lived there, prior to listing it on the market. Focusing on exterior improvements also provided an approved activity where I could spend ample amounts of time outside while on house arrest. Although my electronic bracelet only extended to the mailbox by the curb, it offered just enough space to complete all the outdoor projects I had on my list. Ultimately, landscaping was a way to be productive, while occupying my time and mind.

Karma also approved of the upgrades, since the added time outside meant more time sunbathing for her. For the first time since my head trauma, I felt I was making measurable progress. After a month of landscape improvements, I received notice that I was accepted into the graduate program at Lakeland College.

On May 29, 2014, I started graduate school. I was approximately seven months removed from the TBI.

Part of me felt that I had no business being a graduate student, since I was still struggling with migraines and overall cognitive dysfunction, which included short-term memory loss. The other part of me wanted to prove to myself, and everyone else, that I could prevail over the injury and carve out a career path moving forward.

I devoted every ounce of effort I had into the full-time student schedule, yet I still always felt behind. Everything from studying to writing papers took longer and required more mental energy compared to previous coursework. I recall thinking how school once came easily to me; now, I was forced to utilize maximum effort simply to turn out a short, written assignment.

Even more taxing was my inability to retain new information. I would read a page of text and by the time I completed the page, I had already forgotten a majority of what I just read. In complete frustration, I would re-read page after page, consuming hours of time.

Despite the hours I spent reading, little new information was retained. Instead, old memories encoded prior to the TBI were accessible, whereas everything new seemed to immediately disappear from memory. Part of me felt like I was always living in the past, as those were the only memories I was able to recall. Ask me about something that occurred five years prior, and I could provide an answer. Whereas, recalling something that happened five minutes ago proved to be nearly impossible.

After a month of utter frustration and struggling with memory issues, I applied for medical disability determination through Social Security.

As I waited to hear back from Social Security, I continued to implement different study techniques, hoping something would help me remember. This included playing mind elasticity games specifically designed to improve memory function. Alas, the only reinvented process I was able to "make work" post brain injury was writing papers.

Since graduate school had very few comprehensive tests, much of the emphasis was placed on paper writing and practical learning experiences. For that reason, I was able to complete the first semester. In fact, I received a 4.0 GPA despite my inability to retain a majority of what was being taught.

Overall, I relied on my ability to write and confidently interact with others in scenario-based learning encounters to carry my grades. Participating in counseling role plays, while demonstrating the ability to interact with "clients," literally carried me through the semester. Essentially, I mirrored what I could recall from twelve weeks of Connections IOP groups and did my best to recreate the scenarios in a classroom setting. Overall, my grades reflected my capacity to work within the framework of the courses I was taking, but not my comprehension of the material I was consuming.

Ultimately, I knew I was not going to be able to complete the graduate program without discovering new concepts, but I wanted to try. As I waited on the disability determination, I signed up for another semester of graduate classes. Only this time around, things became more complicated.

CHAPTER 27

PLAYING WITH CHAINS

———

During a two-week hiatus from graduate school, I completed the time I owed on the ankle bracelet.

Immediately following my release from the Jail Diversion program, I added a large forearm tattoo which depicted my interpretation of Lady Justice. In my rendering, Lady Justice still adorns a blindfold, only it serves to block the racism and corruption that plagues the criminal justice system of which she can no longer stomach to view. Furthermore, the sword, which represents enforcement and respect in the original depiction is completely absent. Instead, the arm which is meant to grasp the unsheathed sword is amputated at the elbow, symbolizing justice is broken and without means to administer fair action.

Finally, in my rendition, Justice's scales are filled with a bleeding heart in one dish, and gold coins in the other. The bleeding heart signifies compassion, whereas the gold coins which outweigh the heart, represent money. Ultimately conveying the statement that ample amounts of money, not heart, dictates Lady Justice's level of compassion.

With the statement tattoo complete, I aimed to place my personal relationship with the United States "justice" system behind me.

As summer transitioned into fall, I returned to Lakeland College for a second semester of graduate school. Like the first semester, I continued to struggle with consequences from the TBI. Retaining new information in graduate classes continued to be nearly impossible. Again, I relied heavily upon my ability to write solid papers to carry my grades.

Looking back, I recall feeling like an imposter. Despite the high marks I was receiving, I knew I was not able to remember a majority of what was being taught. Pretending to comprehend lessons, only to forget them prior to leaving the classroom was also exhausting. Ultimately, I concluded that I had little chance of passing future comprehensive exams.

Multiple times per week, I considered dropping out of the program, but my drive to assist others struggling with addiction kept me from quitting. Individuals in recovery seemed to connect with my story and making myself vulnerable before a group inspired others to share. The more I told of my struggles with addiction, the more I saw individuals authentically reveal what they were wrestling to overcome. The act of sharing provided hope I could help prevent someone from making similar mistakes. So, I toiled on.

As I struggled with the demands of graduate school, I decided to return to weightlifting at a new gym. Having lost nearly thirty pounds of muscle mass while incarcerated, I was looking and feeling like a shell of my former self. This impression was reinforced by a closet full of clothing that no longer fit and muscle atrophy that was commented on by everyone close to me during my powerlifting days.

Constantly being told, "you look so skinny," was impacting my already damaged self-esteem, which never truly returned after jail. Overall, I felt like I had lost portions of my mind and body, and only had control over regaining the latter of the two. So, I began working out a minimum of three to four days a week, with the goal of regaining some size and strength. During a bench press workout in early October, eight words uttered by an attractive female trainer would forever change my life.

"You trying to get big playing with chains?"

This was all I heard for a young gym trainer that I had been too shy to approach prior. After completing the heavy set, I was captivated by the bold approach she had taken to start a conversation. Fumbling for a response, I said something along the lines of, "yeah, I'm trying to get big again." She laughed, as did the trainer that was spotting for me, and I was eventually introduced.

Venessa was her name, and I immediately wanted to know more about her. Not only was the 5'3" trainer brave enough to approach me, but she was fearless enough to make a comment that would possibly offend me. I was intrigued.

Over the next few days, I did my best to learn more about Venessa without being labeled "another creepy gym member." During that time, I refused to interrupt her while she worked training clients and tried not to get caught staring at her between sets. Instead, I had a conversation with the manager, whom I often shared commiserating gym stories and found out Venessa came from an extremely close large family. I also discovered that she was about to graduate from UW-Madison and was currently working as a personal trainer to help support her last semester of school.

Aside from that, I learned that Venessa was an elite athlete and walked-on to play Division 1 softball for the Wisconsin Badgers. Overall, I was impressed by all aspects of what I was told about Venessa's life and figured I would ask her out on a date to learn more about her firsthand. Honestly, I had no idea how she would respond, or if she would even consider dating me once she had learned about my past.

It was close to Halloween, so I decided to invite Venessa over to carve pumpkins.

When Venessa came over on October 28, 2014, she immediately bonded with Karma, who was the first to greet her at the door. After about ten minutes of smelling Venessa and receiving pets and rubs, Karma granted her access into the rest of the house and allowed our date to proceed.

Venessa and I carved pumpkins as we talked about life goals. She shared that she was interested in moving to Arizona and had recently applied for an internship with the Arizona State University's Strength and Conditioning Program. I shared how I was in graduate school and was honest about my struggles post brain injury. I also told Venessa about my prior battles with opioid addiction and the long road of legal problems that arose because of it. Venessa listened quietly to everything I had to say without offering an immediate response or reaction. Instead, she seemed to take everything in as she silently weighed her options.

I remember feeling like I "blew it" by completely oversharing on our first date. However, I also felt that anyone getting involved with me had an immediate right to know about my past. Besides, it was the first time I ever told anyone outside of a recovery circle about the wrong I did. I wanted to approach the conversation with absolute transparency.

Fortunately, my risk was rewarded and Venessa agreed to a second date.

Over the next few months, Venessa and I continued to grow as a couple.

In December, we attended one of her friend's weddings together. It was an out of state venue in Florida and marked the first time we traveled together. It was also the first time I met any of Venessa's college friends. Overall, I was impressed by the company that Venessa kept and most of her friend group immediately seemed to accept me. Their acceptance helped me relax and show my authentic self.

Spending time with Venessa made me feel like a person again.

In her companionship, I felt genuinely cared for and supported for the first time in years. Furthermore, Venessa's constant encouragement helped propel me through the daily struggles of living with a traumatic brain injury. In a time where I was still adjusting to what life would offer an individual with brain damage and a criminal record, Venessa treated me with more patience and compassion than I afforded myself.

Instead of simply experiencing life, I began to enjoy aspects of it again.

In the following months, Venessa completed her undergraduate degree and began working at the gym full-time. I finished my second semester of graduate school and seriously began to explore listing my house for sale on the market.

Despite utilizing portions of my student loans to help cover living expenses, I remained financially strapped. Throughout this time of recovery, my mother had continued to help me out financially. While this was extremely caring of her, I felt like I needed to support myself. I owed it to her for all the support she had given me in the past and wanted to stop being a burden on her. Overall, I urgently needed to find a less expensive housing option or supplement the mortgage by adding a roommate.

Venessa again played the role of the savior and agreed to move in sometime during early spring. I was elated and she was convinced that "moving in together would test the strength of our developing relationship." With her assistance, I was able to stay current on the mortgage payments. More importantly, we continued to grow as a couple.

While money remained tight, working together we found a way to make our budget each month. In time, Venessa was promoted at the gym and our financial situation became slightly less dire.

Just as it began to look like we might stay in Madison long-term, Venessa received notification from Arizona State University. She was offered an exclusive internship position with the school's Strength and Conditioning Program starting in fall of 2015.

For her, the situation became even sweeter when her younger sister was accepted for admittance into ASU's incoming freshman class. Overall, it was an absolute dream opportunity for Venessa and one she couldn't pass up.

For me, it meant sell the house or be deprived of the best thing in life aside from Karma. Part of me feared losing the newfound stability that Venessa and I just worked months to create. However, a larger portion was willing to "roll the dice" on relocation simply to continue our journey together. If I could begin to thrive with Venessa in Wisconsin, I certainly could flourish with her under the Arizona sun.

CHAPTER 28

ARIZONA AND ARTWORK

In the fall of 2015, the house went on the market. Listing it was the easiest decision I have ever made. Since Venessa was heading to Arizona to explore the ASU internship, I was willing to give up just about anything to keep her in my life. I was also looking forward to leaving Dane County and a plethora of horrible memories along with it.

Aside from memories made with Venessa, most recollections of my time spent in Dane County revolved around using opioids, being arrested, or recovering from being beaten nearly to death. Almost everywhere I traveled within the city of Madison also shared a negative affiliation to past events. I felt like I couldn't make a single trip outside my home without running into someone that knew the old me.

Despite being a city of over 250,000 people, Madison felt suffocating.

If I were to ever move forward, it was imperative that I do so in a region where I was not reliving past transgressions daily. Hopefully, a change in latitude would result in a change in attitude. I was about to make a nearly 1,700-mile change.

The exterior improvements to the house helped it sell quickly. After some complications with a title lien, which threatened to derail the move entirely, I was finally free from the largest anchor keeping me tethered to the Madison area. Within a couple of days, Venessa and I loaded all our worldly possessions into a POD storage container and set out for Tempe, Arizona.

The cross-country journey was the first major road trip we embarked on together. Unlike the manic Buffalo adventure years prior, this trip was well planned and completely necessary. Venessa turned out to be a wonderful copilot. Not only did she handle the navigation portion of the trip, but also tended to Karma, who required multiple bathroom breaks. Together, the three of us averaged 600 miles per day, and made it to Tempe, Arizona in under three days.

Over the course of the next month, we settled into an apartment located off campus and began to explore our new surroundings. Nearly every day, we made it a point to take Karma to a new dog park or some hiking trail that allowed pets. Karma was absolutely spoiled and possibly loved the climate change most of all. When the heat index broke 100 degrees, Karma lounged in the A/C while Venessa and I spent our time in one of three pools located on the apartment's grounds or lifting weights at the nearby LA Fitness. Overall, we completely embraced the Arizona lifestyle and were just beginning to feel like it would be our forever home when I received a frantic phone call from Wisconsin.

"Have you seen the news?" my mother asked in anguish. "Not today, what's up?" I responded in a nonchalant manner. "You're wanted for stealing a $100,000 painting!" she yelled back into the phone. In the moment I thought she was kidding, "And you're Vincent van Gogh."

Dead silence and I immediately knew my mother was not playing games. "I've got to go; I'll call you back later," I said while turning on our TV. In a few moments, I learned what my mother and viewers across the nation already knew.

On October 29, 2015, a criminal complaint was filed alleging that I stole a painting valued at $100,000 while working for the Capitol Police.

Immediately after the complaint was put on record, the local media in Wisconsin picked up the story and added the words ex-police officer to the narrative. By mid-morning on the same day, my name, along with "ex-police officer in Wisconsin steals one hundred-thousand-dollar painting" was scrolling across the lower portions of televisions screens across the United States. People, including family and friends, tuned into popular morning programming such as the Today Show, saw the headline and immediately began calling my phone. At the time, I was completely caught off-guard, as it had been over four years since I worked for the Capitol Police.

After recovering from the initial shock, I began piecing together information regarding the painting.

While I was working at the Executive Residence, Wisconsin went through a change of governors. In January 2011, Governor James Doyle, who had served eight years, was replaced by newly elected Governor Scott Walker. Prior to moving out of the Executive Residence, the Doyle family purged countless items from the home. These items included numerous promotional gifts the governor received while traveling and performing his executive duties.

Boxes of t-shirts, mugs, hats, posters, etc., were all placed in the basement to be sorted and either donated or thrown away. Prior to the items being donated, staff was permitted to look through the boxes and take whatever they desired, given that they noted exactly what was taken on a paper list that accompanied the soon to be discarded goods. There was also a large, leather bound ledger being utilized by Executive Residence staff to track state owned items that were to remain in the house. Neither I, nor any member of the Dignitary Protection team had access to the ledger, but its existence was meant to help ensure state property was not misplaced.

After waiting a few shifts, I opted to take a new travel mug, a promotional pocketknife, and the painting which was stacked against the wall among posters and other similar items. I was initially attracted to the painting because of its bright, golden frame.

As the son of a former art teacher, I saw my mother re-frame multiple works of art over the years, and I planned to do the same with this piece. I had no idea the small sur-real-style painting, which only measured twelve by sixteen inches, was an original or held any value. After all, the "unique" painting was sitting on the basement floor among donations, not displayed on a wall or locked away in secured storage. For that same reason, I also made no attempt to conceal the painting as I carried it out to my vehicle. Essentially, I believed I was taking a worthless, discarded item.

The Aaron Bohrod painting sat in the bottom of my closet for roughly a month before I looked at it again. At that time, I noticed it had a gallery stamp on the reverse side. This is when I realized the painting likely had some value beyond the frame.

After discovering the possibility of worth, I should have immediately returned it to the Executive Residence. Instead, I researched the artist and discovered, if it were to be authentic, the painting may be worth a couple thousand dollars. I listed the painting for sale online and eventually sold it to a Connecticut based art dealer as an estate sale find for $1,800. This occurred sometime in February 2011.

After I sold the painting, I never thought about it again until the phone call I received from my mother.

I also knew the painting was not worth $100,000 and found it preposterous that the media used such an inflated number.

It wasn't until I read a Wisconsin Journal Article in February 2016, that I learned Joan Sample, a state employee, provided the estimation of value for the piece of artwork. Sample was not an art appraiser but was hired by the Department of Administration to audit and catalog state-owned property at the Executive Residence. According to a statement provided by Sample to the police, the painting was valued at "$100,000 maybe more" and was missing from the security room of the residence.

If Sample's statement was accurate, that would mean a $100,000 piece of artwork was displayed in a dingy security office. Furthermore, I would have had to steal the extremely valuable painting directly from the security office wall without anyone noticing its absence immediately, or for over four years' time. Frankly, her argument made absolutely no sense.

Today, I believe I was accused of stealing the painting because the "historic case" was the last chance for the assistant district attorney in Dane County to charge me with a felony. The grossly inflated value of the painting also guaranteed the case was of felony status and publicized by the media. Additionally, the painting had been for sale at the art gallery in Connecticut for $3,000 for over four years with no interested buyers. Even the dealer that purchased the painting stated he would "probably give it an insurance value of $5,000." Ultimately, if the painting would have been appraised at $3,000 or less, the crime would have been considered a misdemeanor instead of a felony.

Instead, I faced multiple felony changes and if convicted could serve up to twenty-one years in prison!

As the court case slowly proceeded, I was forced to take a flight from Arizona to Wisconsin for each required appearance. Typically, I would stay in Wisconsin at Venessa's mother house for approximately one night, go to court, then fly back to Arizona. Plane tickets alone ended up costing thousands of dollars as the proceedings dragged on.

After making four round trips and spending thousands more on legal representation, I eventually agreed to a plea deal on April 4, 2016. Having hemorrhaged money for months, I could no longer afford to fight against the trumped-up charges. I was also unwilling to risk up to twenty-one years of my life in prison over a misplaced painting. Ultimately, I had no choice but to plead guilty and the prosecuting attorney knew that from the start.

While researching this case, I came across an interesting article from the Hartford Courant. Within the article, the daughter of artist Aaron Bohrod, who painted the "Gold Fantasy Box" was interviewed. According to the daughter, "her father used to say how badly his feelings were hurt when, earlier in his career, a thief broke into his art studio and stole only his frames—leaving all his paintings behind," (Bell, 2016). Thankfully, I was not yet born when that theft occurred, or I would have likely been charged for that crime as well.

Today, I find it sadly coincidental that the fine framework which attracted me to Bohrod's painting was determined to be the only thing worth stealing from his studio years ago. The article went on to state the daughter, "wishes she (Sample) would appraise all his artwork" (Bell, 2016), noting that many of the paintings remain in the family's possession.

To date, Bohrod's "Gold Fantasy Box" continues to haunt me. A simple internet search of my name immediately yields an unflattering mugshot coupled with the story of how I stole the $100,000 painting. Since the articles regarding the stolen painting were published, I've found it nearly impossible to obtain work at a living wage. Couple the unfavorable articles with a felony label and potential employers are even more hesitant to consider me for an interview.

Ultimately, the painting, and the mug shot comprise the totality of factors by which most people formulate their first, and often only impression of me. A hiring manager even remarked that I was, "remarkably kind and well-spoken for someone with such an extensive criminal record." I was not hired for that opening.

I do not believe I am a unique case regarding the power of past transgressions, especially those paired with a felony label, and their ability to completely derail future hopes of living a prosperous, reformed life.

Instead, I believe most felons are never again "given the benefit of the doubt" or provided a fair working alternative once the indefinite label is in place. These forever labels, not current actions, continue to dictate a felon's worth to society even decades after the original crime was committed. Once a felon discovers they hold little value to, or a greatly diminished chance of productively operating within societal constructs, they become more likely to recidivate.

As someone who has lived with the felony label for over six years, I can attest that very few privileges remain after acquiring the devastating tag.

CHAPTER 29

MILK AND SNOW

———

Nobody wants to go back to the land of milk and snow. That is what I was thinking when I attended a plea hearing in late June of 2016. Despite knowing that I would be entering a guilty plea, I was not psychologically ready to abandon a fresh start in Arizona in exchange for a return to Wisconsin to face sentencing.

During the plea agreement process, I agreed to serve ten months jail time paired with four years of felony probation, in exchange for pleading guilty to stealing the Aaron Bohrod painting. More importantly, by agreeing to the plea bargain, I avoided the possibility of spending twenty-one years in prison should I have fought the case in court and lost. As I previously mentioned, the gamble of twenty-one years was too great of a risk to contest the theft charge and overall value of the painting.

Ultimately, the threat of the maximum penalty persuaded me to take the plea deal. Reflecting upon it now, I think that was the prosecutor's goal all along; scare me into accepting a plea deal knowing the risk of fighting the charges outweighed the benefits of trying the case. I was also completely out of funds to continue the legal battle, so the prosecutor's plan worked. In the end, it was an easy victory to secure.

Utterly defeated, it was agreed upon that I would return to Wisconsin for sentencing on August 8, 2016.

Prior to returning to Wisconsin, I aimed to live my best life in Arizona. Over the course of two months, Venessa, Karma, and I went on multiple hiking excursions. Our favorite was to remote Greer, AZ where we stayed in a cabin and tackled hiking trails ranging between 8,000 and 9,000 feet of elevation. Greer also offered some of the most beautiful landscape views, which made the rigorous hikes worth the reward. For me, our trip to Greer will forever remain the highlight from an overall adventure cut too short. Aside from hiking, we also added another member to our family while living under the Arizona sun.

Titan, a black and silver German Shepherd puppy, found his forever home one afternoon while we were shopping in an Arizona mall. Venessa, who picked up a job to help support our financial needs at Arizona's largest Humane Society, had been interested in adding a canine companion for Karma for several months. Although she saw countless surrenders at the Humane Society, we were looking for a moldable puppy to train alongside Karma and hopefully inherit her best traits. I was also looking to certify our next dog as an emotional support animal and a puppy was our best option.

When we first saw Titan, he immediately stood out to us because he had giant "radar" ears. The poor puppy with giant ears reminded me of the story of Dumbo, especially the way he was displayed in the center of the pet store. After talking to the shop owner, I discovered that Titan was being viewed by upwards of seventy people per day. The overwhelmed puppy spent most of his existence subjected to selfies and being temporarily loved in 15-minute intervals. Much like I could not leave Karma chained to a tree, I could not leave Titan in the middle of a crowded mall pet store.

After haggling over the price, while Venessa played with Titan in an adjacent room, I eventually came to a workable number. Venessa had no idea I made the purchase until I returned to the room and told her "Pick him up and let's go." Venessa began to cry and remained in complete disbelief until the pet store owner joined us with a receipt and Titan's paperwork. Today, Titan remains the best mall purchase I have ever made.

As the three of us became four, we continued to enjoy Arizona right until the day we left.

On August 8, 2016, I returned to Wisconsin for sentencing. The plea bargain deal was honored by the judge, and I was given sixty days to "get my life in order" before reporting to Dane County Jail. The extended timetable allowed me to apply to the Jail Diversion Program and avoid returning directly to jail.

Furthermore, I was able to reapply for Social Security disability after being denied the first time through the process. Essentially, I needed to prove I attempted to work after my TBI. The failure to complete graduate school did not count toward that endeavor. I recall feeling helpless by the forced return to Wisconsin and the rejection letter from Social Security made matters worse. As our return date to Wisconsin rapidly approached, I began to slide into a serious depression.

Self-doubt became my greatest nemesis reflecting upon relocating back to Wisconsin. From prior experience, I knew that I could survive ten months on the ankle bracelet, but I was not looking forward to daily isolation. Despite having

Venessa and the two dogs to accompany me, being placed back on house arrest meant months of disconnection from the outside world. In Arizona, I maximized every opportunity to express my freedom and partake in whatever adventure arose. Meanwhile, in Wisconsin, I would only be able to travel outside my house for work purposes, which I wasn't even sure I would be capable of doing.

I was scared shitless of the thought of not being able to consistently contribute to a future place of employment. After all, I wasn't retaining much in the way of new information, and I was still dealing with multifactorial cognitive dysfunction coupled with debilitating migraines multiple times per week. There was also the issue of money, or lack thereof, which drove my anxiety further.

Since Venessa and I were living paycheck to paycheck, we had very little money to make the return trip to Wisconsin. We exhausted all our savings on my flights and legal fees, so there was literally no money to fall back on. The last remaining item of value I owned was my vehicle, a small BMW SUV. To raise enough money for the return move to Wisconsin, along with a temporary cushion for us to reestablish within the state, I sold the BMW a couple weeks before leaving Arizona.

While the sale carried us financially, it felt like I was giving up the last tangible piece of my "free" life. I was never upset by the sale of the vehicle, but I was unhappy with forfeiting another symbol of my freedom. Since my teenage years, I maintained ownership of a vehicle and relied heavily upon the privilege possessing one provided. Losing that freedom made me feel trapped, similar to how I felt living with my father prior to receiving the keys to my first car. Selling my car, just like accepting the plea deal, limited my ability to choose our next destination.

Soon I would be confined to invisible perimeters monitored by an electronic ankle bracelet.

CHAPTER 30

FELONY PROBATION

———

During the first week of October 2016, I began serving four years of felony probation.

Unlike the failed misdemeanor probation, this time around I was fully committed to completing the higher stakes felony probation.

From the day I first reported, I was honest and transparent with my probation agent. I informed her of my past addiction to opioids, along with my more recent struggles post-traumatic brain injury. I explained how Venessa and our two dogs comprised an integral support system and that their love would help keep me dedicated to successfully completing probation.

Overall, I could tell the senior agent was skeptical, but willing to listen to what I had to say. She jotted down a few notes and asked for medical verification regarding the TBI. Next, she reviewed a list of rules spanning over two pages. I signed my life away and the four-year countdown clock began.

My first task on probation was to find employment. Not only did I need to be employed to leave the house while on jail diversion, but it was also a requirement imposed by the court. Searching for employment with a felony conviction, however, proved to be nearly impossible.

Despite having a bachelor's degree, I was immediately disqualified from several jobs based solely on my criminal record. Furthermore, after selling my vehicle in Arizona, I was without reliable transportation. As a result, my prospect as a potential job candidate was at an all-time low. To even be considered for a position, I needed to improve my worth. Just as I began to lose all confidence regarding my employability, a landscape company responded to my application.

After a brief interview, I was hired as a general laborer for the local landscape company. The work was literally described as backbreaking, but I had no other employment options. I also had no way of getting to my new place of employment, despite telling them otherwise during my interview. Just as I thought I was going to have to rescind the accepted offer, Cesar called out of the blue to see how I was doing. As I explained my transportation situation, he offered to allow me to borrow a vehicle he was not using as a daily driver.

Just like he did in the jail pod, Cesar bailed me out of what looked to be a dire situation. Later that evening, he showed up at my door with the keys to a Mustang convertible. Cesar is a true friend.

With transportation secured, I began working for the landscape company. The work was as grueling as promised, but that did not deter me from working hard to verify I was a solid hire. Instead, it was the sounds of the job that proved to be most challenging.

Throughout the day, I was assaulted by noise. Leaf blowers, lawn mowers, and other mechanical equipment operating at high decibels rattled my nerves. Typically, I could push through until lunch, that is when the migraine would hit.

Pain built up in my head until I could barely see. While I continued working, the internal pressure kept building and building. Soon vertigo would follow, making it hard for me to stand. On multiple occasions, I would get to my feet, only to rush for a bucket to vomit into.

Prior to the head injury, I never suffered a true migraine and ultimately equated them to a bad headache. Only after I began experiencing them did I realize how debilitating they could be. Each migraine day I entered a personal hell. The pounding in the surgically repaired left side of my face literally brought me to tears. I remember telling coworkers I had seasonal allergies, to cover for the regular afternoon waterworks.

Despite the migraines and vertigo, I continued to work for the landscape company until winter layoffs hit sometime in mid-November. It was the first time in my life that I was seasonally laid off, and I was grateful.

After the seasonal downsizing, I shifted my attention toward receiving additional medical attention for the migraines. At the time, I was also suffering from insomnia, which seemed to get worse as my general anxiety levels increased. Once I talked to my primary doctor, I was again referred to neuropsychology for further testing and diagnosis. A neurology and headache team confirmed the migraine symptoms, along with a "mental disorder due to known physiological condition."

As the team began to explore the mental health side of things further, I was also diagnosed with major depressive disorder. The visit ultimately resulted in me being placed on a handful of medications to help treat the migraines, along with generalized anxiety and depression. I was also told to avoid work situations that triggered the migraines, specifically working in loud environments for extended periods of time. So, I began to search for another job.

Within a month, I began working at Goodwill. There I was responsible for collecting and sorting donations. The migraine medication, along with the reduced noise levels, provided some relief. I was able to reduce my overall migraine days to a couple per week.

Sadly, the Goodwill position was only able to offer "near full-time hours" and the pay was a dismal $10.10 per hour. Although I was grateful to be employed, the low hourly wage barely provided enough income to cover my monthly expenses. Furthermore, because the position was only part-time, it did not offer health insurance benefits.

I quickly found myself in a position where I made slightly too much money to qualify for low-income health care coverage, but not enough to afford a monthly premium on my own. Fortunately, Venessa was also working, and our combined income covered our essential needs. However, I went without healthcare for a handful of months while working for Goodwill. During that time frame, I felt powerless to improve my situation. Depression continued to gain control.

Between sleepless nights and unshakable depression, I began to feel like my life was never going to improve. For the first time in my existence, I truly questioned if I would have the strength to continue to carry on. Recurring thoughts of suicide infiltrated my leisure time, and I began to convince myself that the world would be a better place without me.

I recall only being able to focus on the negative. Self-pity consumed anything that otherwise would have brought me joy. Similar to when I relapsed, I would unwillingly go two to three days without sleeping. As I neared my breaking point, I would eventually "crash and burn." To me, this meant falling asleep out of pure exhaustion. After I finally got to sleep, the process would repeat itself.

One, two, three days of little to no sleep, followed by a distinctive crash.

Then one night, when I thought things couldn't possibly get any worse, I heard a disembodied voice.

CHAPTER 31

PSYCHOSIS

The first time I ever heard a "voice", I thought I had completely lost my mind.

I was lying in bed, completely sober, when a distinct voice broke through the silence. The voice itself sounded angry, almost demonic. It called out as if it were coming from behind and above me all at the same time. At first, I tried to dismiss it as sounds from the neighbor's television set, but the enraged voice was persistent. Again, it broke the silence of the night and again I tried to offer some justification for what I had just heard.

As justifications gave way to fear, I woke Venessa up. In a panic, I asked her to listen for a voice and tell me what she heard. Half asleep, she must have thought I was crazy until she saw the tears welling up in my eyes. She listened for a while and told me she did not hear anything. Then she asked, "what are you hearing?" I responded with two words, "red monkey", which together meant absolutely nothing to me. I told Venessa that I heard the words repeated twice and I was certain it came from within our bedroom. As Venessa tried to comfort me, I heard the voice once more, this time certain she heard it as well.

When she still heard nothing, I told her, "I think I'm going crazy."

After another sleepless night, Venessa and I spoke more about the voice again the next morning. I told her it was the first time I had ever heard it or anything remotely like it. As she offered potential origins for the "sound", internally, I knew it was something more.

What scared me the most was the authenticity of the overall experience. Although I could not explain what uttered the two-word phrase, I was certain something or someone had spoken. To comprehend the event, I began to utilize Venessa as a "voice indicator" by frequently asking her to name and identify what sounds she was hearing. When her sounds corresponded to mine, I eventually wrote the event off as a one-time brain malfunction. Perhaps it was simply the lack of sleep that caused me to hear the voice. Regardless of the cause, I did my best to continue as if nothing ever happened.

Over the next month, I left my position at Goodwill and began working for a plumbing company. The plumbing company offered better hourly pay, along with health benefits after ninety days of employment. My goal was to make it through the short probationary period, obtain health insurance, and reconnect with mental health services. I knew that without health insurance, we could not afford to pay for counseling, nor any medication that was likely to be prescribed. So, I began to grind through each painstaking day, one hour at a time.

Most days, I was able to conceal my mental instability by focusing on the task at hand. I refused to allow myself to think about anything outside of work and envisioned my body as a machine meant to perform a particular task. This process worked at first, until I heard a voice at work.

Unlike the demonic voice, the one I heard while water piping the basement of a new house sounded more like whispers. I could not make out what the whispers were saying, and they reminded me of static playing over the radio. At times, a loud, buzzing noise would accompany the static murmurs. I tried everything I could to drown out the noise, including listening to blaring music, but nothing worked.

Again, it was as if the whispers were generated around and above me. They also made it extremely difficult to focus on conversation. For example, the journeyman I worked under would be explaining a task, and his voice would have to compete with the muttered static I was hearing inside my head. It reminded me of attempting to filter out white noise, while trying to pick out the words with meaning. It was nearly impossible to navigate, but I pretended like everything was normal.

I worked with the sporadic whispers for three months, without saying a thing to anyone aside from Venessa. She was the only one I trusted enough to share the actual truth with, until I was able to see a trained medical professional. Together, we counted down the days until I was eligible for the company's health insurance plan. Venessa could tell I was coming undone and in desperate need of medical intervention. She did her best to play substitute counselor, while I continued to battle the voices in my head.

In January 2018, after barely clinging to sanity for three months, I finally saw a mental health professional. After a screening appointment, I was diagnosed with having generalized anxiety disorder along with major depressive disorder. The two diagnoses were similar to the mental health diagnosis I had in the past, and I was placed on a daily anxiety medication along with something to help me sleep.

Despite being transparent and explaining the disembodied voices during the screening and to the attending social worker, no action was taken to address their presence. Instead, it seemed the doctor preferred to treat only what he immediately understood and referred me to a Neurology and Headache team for the rest. Even Venessa tried to advocate for more immediate treatment, but nothing else was done. From this point forward, my overall health continued to diminish.

About a month after receiving the mental health diagnosis, I began experiencing horrible stomach issues. Daily diarrhea suddenly became an issue, and I found myself in the bathroom upwards to a dozen times per day. Unlike the mental health issues, I could not hide the need to consistently go to the bathroom from my coworkers. Fearful that I would lose my plumbing job due to constant bathroom breaks, I sought medical intervention to help explain my sudden gastrointestinal issues.

By the first week in March, I was scheduled for a colonoscopy along with a biopsy. The results of the biopsy came back negative, but it was found that I had a form of colitis.

It felt like my mind and body were betraying me all at once.

Just as things looked like they could not get any worse, we discovered a mass on the back of one of Karma's legs. Venessa, who was now working at an animal hospital, got her in for immediate treatment. The mass, which was roughly the size of a dime, was surgically removed and a biopsy was performed. After waiting a few days for the results, we discovered that the mass was cancerous.

Additional testing revealed the cancer had already spread to Karma's lymph nodes. When the veterinarian shared this information with us, I basically broke. The thought of losing Karma, on top of being sick myself, was too much for me to take. Venessa stepped up and discussed treatment options, while I did my best just to remain present. I knew no matter which treatment avenue we decided upon, I had limited time to spend with my best friend. The vet told us we had weeks, possibly months, depending on how quickly the cancer spread throughout the rest of Karma's body. As much as I wanted to be strong and resilient, I was consumed by depression and the feeling that life was continually getting worse.

In the months that followed, Karma got sicker and so did I.

We both began having accidents. My stomach got so bad that I had to leave work early one day after I didn't make it off a roof in time to use a Porta Potty. I remember the incident, because I felt humiliated having to tell another grown man that I needed to leave work because "I shit myself." I remember calling my mom and crying the entire ride home. Despite my mother's support, I continued on a mental health backslide.

At the time, it seemed like the more Karma struggled, the more I broke down. My sleep became even more erratic, and I began hearing both voices more frequently. The more I heard the voices, the more I began to question reality. It all became a vicious cycle.

Within a few weeks, I completely lost hold of being able to manage all my symptoms coupled with the demands of daily life. The only place I felt secure was in our bedroom's walk-in closet. I began calling into work just to seek shelter there during the day. Karma used to curl up next to me, as I positioned my back against the wall, physically shaking with tears streaming from my eyes.

I was so ashamed of my inability to "hold it together" that I didn't even tell Venessa I was calling in sick. Every time I tried to tell her, I let self-made fear get in the way. Anxiety was getting the best of me, and I ruminated on the worst-case scenario of Venessa leaving me. Instead of having another difficult conversation, I laid next to Karma, tried to ignore the intrusive voices, and longed for better days.

CHAPTER 32

HOSPITALIZATION

On July 24, 2018, I experienced several "firsts" in my life. It was the first time I'd written a suicide note. It was also the first time I confided in someone besides Venessa regarding the voices in my head. Finally, it was the first time I trusted a branch of the criminal justice system to listen to me and do what was morally right.

Between Karma's cancer diagnosis and intermittently hearing inexplicable voices for several months, I couldn't take anymore. Mentally, I was as unhinged as I had ever been and hope for improvement was all but lost. I began thinking in only absolutes. For example, I believed the voices that I was hearing were going to continue to torment me for the rest of my life. By thinking in this manner, I already conceded victory to a mental illness that I had only begun fighting.

Although it wasn't in my nature to give up, I felt so exhausted by pretending to be alright, that I didn't have the energy to continue to advocate for myself when it mattered most. Instead of turning it over to someone that could help, I allowed shame and a feeling of worthlessness to override my thoughts of sharing. I kept everything bottled up within, until one day, I literally wanted to cut it all out.

Tactical knife at my side, I began writing a suicide note to Venessa. In the note, I thanked her for always seeing the best in me and apologized for not being strong enough to overcome the voices. I also asked her to continue to care for Karma and Titan, but especially Karma, since her time was nearing an end. I told her how much I loved her and how I no longer wished to be a burden to her or anyone else.

Everything I was writing in that moment was "me" centric. I could no longer see beyond my daily hardships and struggles. As I tried to find the perfect words to summarize the remaining reasons why I was about to take my life, Karma began to nuzzle her head underneath my arm. Looking down at her, I realized she was trying to divert my attention for one reason or another. The interruption caused me to stop writing and refocus my awareness toward her needs. Within seconds, Karma was at the door indicating she needed to go outside.

In the time it took for me to take Karma outside to use the bathroom, I began to reframe my thoughts.

Did I really want Venessa to come home to find me dead? How would the people that loved me respond to me taking my own life?

As soon as I started looking outside myself, I began finding unsettling answers to questions I did not want to contemplate. The shame and guilt I internalized realigned to reflect how my suicide would make others feel. In that moment, Karma helped me pause, just long enough to realize how selfish the act of taking my own life would be.

Karma's presence saved my life.

By the time we were back inside, I needed an alternative plan to help me survive the day. Without hesitation, I called my probation agent and alerted her to my dire situation.

After listening to me recap the morning's events, my agent requested that I immediately come to her office. As I drove across town to meet her, I contemplated turning around multiple times. I was afraid that being honest with my agent was going to result in me being locked away on a mandatory psychiatric hold. Although I knew I needed mental health intervention, I wanted to receive it on my own terms. Just as I thought I made a mistake calling her, I pulled up to the probation and parole office.

Inside the office, I was greeted by my agent and two female police officers. I instantly had flashbacks to when I was arrested while working for UW Police Department. Recalling how poorly I was treated by the police, made me apprehensive to openly share the mental health crisis I was experiencing. When my agent asked that I "repeat what I told her over the phone in front of the two officers," I instantly hesitated. I knew that if not chosen carefully, my next words would likely result in a minimum seventy-two-hour mental health hold.

Instead, I told the officers that I was merely contemplating suicide and that I needed help. I left out the part about writing Venessa a suicide note, and my plan to utilize a tactical knife to end my life. Alternatively, I explained, "I'm willing to check into a hospital immediately if it's guaranteed I receive psychiatric care." I also clarified, "I want to self-commit in order to gain more autonomy over my care." One of the officers was surprisingly empathetic to my story and agreed that "the hospital was the safest place for me." Within minutes, I was transported from the probation office to UW Hospital.

Once we arrived at the hospital, the same officer agreed to wait with me until I was completely checked in. As we waited, she told me stories about her son and how as a mother she would be grateful if her son sought help in a similar situation. She went on to share that she was pursuing her master's degree in counseling and would be leaving the police force in the next year or so.

As we talked, I opened up to Officer Alex Nieves. I told her about the voices I was hearing, along with how I was calling in sick to work to "hide in a walk-in closet, the only place I felt safe." Office Nieves listened without judging and assured me that mental health staff at the hospital would help me in any way they could.

Despite being a police officer, it was her motherly presence that kept me calm and rational. Once I was finally checked-in, Officer Nieves gave me a hug and provided her name and phone number should I ever find myself in need again. Her professionalism, coupled with the act of authentically caring, helped re-insure me that I could recover inside the hospital walls.

Once I was a patient inside the secure mental health floor, I began treatment by focusing on the essentials such as eating, attending physical therapy sessions, and getting ample sleep. After a couple days, I had the basics down. Self-care was added to my routine, and I was allowed to have a visitor.

During visitation, I discussed the suicide note with Venessa. Together, we developed a safety plan in case I ever found myself contemplating taking my own life again. Everything I did while hospitalized was aimed at returning me to a functioning baseline. After two nights of quality sleep, and the introduction of two new medications, the voices subsided.

Without the voices interrupting throughout the day, I was able to start differentiating between fact and fiction. I learned how to function without utilizing Venessa as a guide. Reconnected with reality, I was able to learn more about the voices and potential triggers for them. At last, my condition, which I considered to be insanity, had a name.

The hospital diagnosed me with psychosis.

Psychosis, a severe mental disorder, remains the most challenging phenomenon I have encountered. Even though I had been pushed to the edge battling my addiction with pills, that was nothing in comparison. While suffering from psychosis, I completely lost my understanding of reality. After losing the ability to discriminate actuality from perceived reality, I also lost the ability to function within society. The unmanaged psychosis nearly resulted in me taking my own life. Today, I avoid the damning symptoms of psychosis with medication, as well as sleep and anxiety regulation.

Once stable, I also discovered a correlation between the number of repeated days of inadequate sleep and the voices I was experiencing. Essentially, if my sleep becomes broken for two to three consecutive days, the risk of psychosis becomes much greater. Furthermore, if my anxiety becomes unmanageable, that too can drive the psychosis. Overall, managing the triggers that cause my psychosis is the only true way to avoid another mental collapse. Without structure and proper medication, the psychosis could easily return.

However, as I came to realize during a second hospitalization, mental health isn't always as transparent as it seems.

CHAPTER 33

LOSING MY BEST FRIEND

While I was hospitalized, we received a letter from Social Security Disability. After years of applying and being denied, I was finally approved for complete and total disability on July 24, 2018.

The biggest take away from the approval letter was I would begin receiving monthly disability compensation. Although the amount was only a percentage of what I was once capable of earning, it was enough to ensure that I didn't have to continue to pretend to be fully-functioning while trying to maintain work. Furthermore, I would no longer be required by probation to sustain employment since I was classified as completely disabled.

Verification letter in hand, I could finally put aside the facade and begin to live within the constraints of my physiological condition. Furthermore, I could utilize the new label to name what those closest to me already knew. While I survived the beating from the Maglite, a part of me never got back up off the concrete. A portion of me was genuinely "fully disabled."

As I began to embrace the new label, I spent most of my days at home with Karma and Titan. Karma, who continued to fight against cancer, slept most days away. Sporadically, she would have an active day, where we would go for a short walk next to the nearby pond. However, most days she was content just lying in the sun on our apartment's balcony. Titan and I typically matched Karma's energy throughout the day. Neither of us pushed the matriarch to do more than she was capable of in the moment. Overall, we were both content with just letting her do whatever she wanted to do. After all, she was fighting an internal battle each day that neither of us could see. Then one evening in mid-October, Karma's fight came to an end.

While I've written about my own pain throughout this memoir, the pain of losing Karma is something I still struggle to cope with almost daily. A simple mention of a memory we shared will bring tears to my eyes and often force me to redirect the conversation. When I reflect upon the impact that Karma had on my life, I cannot begin to express the gratitude I owe her for the unconditional love and loyalty she provided.

Karma was once my everything and the only thing that kept me persevering in times where I wanted to give up. It was her fighter's spirit that I borrowed from and her ability to overcome the worst of the human condition that made me believe I too could survive. Even when I felt abandoned for my wrongdoings, Karma continued to greet me with great enthusiasm. She showed me how to love and she showed me how to fight.

My life without Karma would have ended years ago.

As I think of her, I'm reminded of how fortunate I am to be the one to have rescued her from that tree. Little did I know at the time, she would repay me countless times over. Just like her paw print memorial tattoo is etched into my skin, Karma's legacy remains carved into my heart. I'll never find another friendship like hers, but I'm blessed to have ever known a relationship so pure.

As the tears stream from my eyes and down my face, I am reminded that Karma was so much more than a household pet. As her namesake indicates, she was destined for greatness after her initial state of existence was so deplorable. Today, Karma's memory serves as a reminder of how life with love should be lived.

After Karma's passing, everyone in our household experienced some form of depression. Titan temporarily lost his zest for life and gained a few pounds while grieving the motherly figure that raised him. Venessa did her best to keep the men in her life stable and was unable to truly mourn for months after Karma's passing. I slipped deep into a depression that knew no depths and joined a NAMI, the National Alliance of Mental Illness, support group.

However, no matter what therapeutic tools I implemented; I simply could not shake the major depressive state I entered after Karma died. Sorrow and guilt over lost time devoured me. After months of struggling, I was hospitalized again.

On April 3, 2019, I was admitted into UW Hospital for mental health needs for a second time in roughly eight months. This time around I was not suicidal but was so depressed that I stopped eating and abandoned most other forms of self-care. Prior to the hospitalization, Venessa and I reviewed the safety plan I completed during my first stay and found we could place check marks in nearly all the warning boxes. This indicated that I needed professional help and I agreed to voluntarily check into inpatient treatment. I knew the only way I stood a chance at defeating the severe depression was with professional intervention likely paired with some form of medication.

Since I was in a more stable state when compared to my first visit, the mental health team was immediately able to begin talk therapy regarding my current disorder. As I spoke with different professionals in the mental health field, I was able to begin documenting a history of bipolar like behaviors throughout my life. While we explored these behaviors further over the course of my three-day stay, I also shared a family history of bipolar depression.

After explaining why I believed I was suffering from bipolar disorder to a group of doctors, I was provided new medication geared toward its specific treatment. While the medication would take four to six weeks to load in my system, the fact that my mental health concerns were immediately being heard and addressed helped lift my spirits slightly.

After years of advocating for treatment and trying to comprehend what was "wrong" with me, I finally found an explanation that fit both personally and medically. Prior to being released from the hospital on April 5th, my mental health diagnosis was changed from major depressive disorder with psychosis, to bipolar disorder with psychosis.

For me, the modified diagnosis immediately resulted in a long overdue change to how I was going to be treated. Instead of focusing on single symptoms associated with bipolar depression, the doctors switched gears to better mediate my rollercoaster like mood swings. As the medication loaded in my system, I was paired with a counselor and psychiatrist to work through the transition. Ultimately, the duo collaborated to provide comprehensive treatment and I began making progress toward depression recovery.

As the Summer of 2019 approached, I viewed life through a completely new lens.

CHAPTER 34

GRACE

———

"Bang, bang, bang." Our household awoke to a fist colliding with the front door.

Startled by the early morning interruption, I scrambled for my cell phone to see what time it was. The digital clock display showed sometime after 2 a.m. on a hot July night. Before I could make my way out of bed, Titan was at the door, growling in response to the late-night caller.

His growl quickly became a warning bark as the unidentified visitor pulled open the creaking screen door. Upon hearing the additional commotion, I stopped at the hallway closet and armed myself with a machete. If someone was coming through the door, they were going to have to get through Titan and me.

"Bang, bang, bang," three additional hard knocks against the storm door indicated the potential intruder was still on the other side.

Recalling the room clearing exercises from my dignitary protection days, I tactically moved past the "fatal funnel," or area directly in front of the door, to an adjacent wall. From my new vantage point, I called out, "Who's there?" I could feel my heart pounding in my chest as I awaited a response.

Suddenly, in a slurred tone, a voice responded unintelligibly. Between Titan's barking and the individual talking through the front door, I could hardly hear what the person was saying. Again, I asked, "Who's there?" This time I was able to make out some of the words. "Bro, please let me in."

I cracked the front door just enough to see the face of our neighbor's son. He was holding the screen door open with one hand and a third of a 1.75 liter of Tito's Vodka in the other. He was clearly inebriated and appeared to be using the opened door as a prop to keep himself upright.

Immediately, he started in on a story of how he lost his cell phone in our front bushes and needed help to find it. In exchange, he offered me the remainder of the Vodka, along with "all the money he had on him." As he began to search his pockets, I closed the front door and told him, "Wait here while I get a flashlight." Realizing the intoxicated college student meant no immediate harm, I put down the machete, gathered a flashlight, and joined him in the search for his missing cell.

Together, we looked through the trampled down landscape just outside of the master bedroom window. As we searched, the neighbor informed me he desperately needed his cell phone because, "his mom locked him out of the house, and he needed to call a friend for a place to stay." I asked him for his cell phone number to call the missing phone, but he was too intoxicated to provide the digits.

Eventually, we found the discarded cell phone in a patch of wet foliage. I disregarded the notion that he likely urinated in the area, and possibly on the phone, and instructed him to call his friend. While he called, I went into the backyard and got him a lawn chair to sit on. I placed the lawn chair in the front yard of his mother's house and told him to take a seat. Since he seemed safe until his friend's arrival, I went back into our house and locked the door.

By this time, Venessa was wide awake and wondering what the hell was going on. She got up to use the bathroom as I caught her up to speed. While she was in the bathroom, we heard the same pounding noise, only this time at the backdoor. Venessa yelled from the bathroom window something to the effect of, "dude, you've got to figure this out." The drunken fool replied, "fuck you bitch!" as I made my way toward the backdoor.

This time around, I pulled the door open without warning. After nearly falling through the doorway, the neighbor immediately began apologizing for his language. Slightly aggravated, I asked him about the status of his friend.

He told me, "I called, but he won't come... so I threw my phone again." Again, I helped him find his phone, got him a bottle of water, and we returned to the lawn chair in his mother's front lawn. By this time, it was almost 3 a.m. and I was running out of patience. I told him, "Call your friend and give me the phone."

As the neighbor sat in the lawn chair, I explained the situation to his friend. I told him that "his friend needed his help immediately" and was "too drunk to make good decisions." I also explained that Venessa had work in the morning, and we could not afford to be interrupted again. The friend thanked me for not calling the police and promised to pick his friend up within the next fifteen minutes.

Next, I explained everything to the inebriated neighbor, who again offered me "all his money and Vodka." After receiving a guarantee that he "wouldn't bother us again," I wished my neighbor the best of luck with the rest of his evening. Finally, I went back inside and joined Venessa in our bed.

The next morning, I awoke to find the remainder of the Vodka bottle, along with thirty cents in change on our front porch. The landscape outside our bedroom window was destroyed, including a shrub that I recently pruned. Although I was upset about the landscaping, I was more concerned with the condition of our neighbor.

The chair I lent him the night before was still in the front yard, but he was nowhere to be found. I hoped his friend picked him up as promised, as I took inventory to see if anything else was damaged. When everything else looked to be in order, I returned the chair to our backyard and went about with my day.

Later that afternoon, the young man's mother saw Venessa return home from work and immediately engaged in conversation. She apologized for her son's actions and explained to Venessa that, "he just lost a full scholarship to UW-Madison and was taking it very hard." She also expressed gratitude that we did not call the police and gave Venessa a heartfelt hug to back up the sentiment.

Venessa explained that we "would never call the police unless it was a true emergency." She also empathized with the mother over her son's difficulties. Although the conversation only lasted a couple minutes, it was long enough for the two women to bond over what could have been a horrible situation. As they spoke outside, I remained inside and reflected upon my actions.

The evening prior, I was given the chance to act in a better way. In a moment when a near stranger desperately needed someone to intervene, I responded by mediating with that individual's best interest in mind. Perhaps I saw a bit of my younger self in him and that increased my willingness to help.

Would it have been easier to simply call the police, or smash his face in as was once done to me? What point would be proven by beating an already defeated individual?

As an alternative to choosing violence, I put myself in his shoes. As an individual that has needed help countless times over, I viewed the moment as my time to return the favor. As a substitute to seeing a fucked-up individual, I saw someone that was fucked-up and in need of help. In a world where so much comes down to perception, I placed precedent on my ability to perceive another's need for assistance.

My life with Karma taught me that how we respond to situations typically determines the overall outcome. By responding with grace, we can treat one another with equality and justice. Through the act of providing undeserved love, we can change one's outcome, and potentially their individual narrative moving forward.

If only I could thank Karma one last time for giving me the courage to take that first step. Her unconditional love provided a reason to keep putting one foot in front of the other. She gave me the strength to continue my journey when all I wanted to do was lay down and quit. While moving forward has proven to be the most difficult course of action, Karma showed me that just a moment of kindness can start you on that path.

ACKNOWLEDGMENTS

First and foremost, I would like to thank my wife Venessa. Your unwavering support kept me determined in times when I didn't think completing this memoir would be possible. Your patience throughout the entire process was saintly and your unconditional love fueled me from start to finish. Without you, I would have never had the strength to relive this journey, let alone document it for the world to read.

I would also like to thank my family for helping me narrate my side of the story. Pestering me to write a book over the last four years has finally paid off. I cannot thank you enough for the consistent encouragement and support you have shown over the years.

Additional thanks to the UW Hospital, Connections Counseling, and NAMI of Dane County for providing medical, counseling, and peer services to continue my path to recovery.

Thank you to Eric Koester, Georgetown Professor and Founder of the Creator Institute, for providing the tools and connections I needed to thrive. Thank you to my publisher, New Degree Press, for taking a chance on a cop, turned criminal, turned author. Additionally, thank you Chuck Oexmann who acted as both mentor and coach.

An extended thank you to everyone mentioned in this book, regardless of context, for being part of my life and teaching me something along the way.

Finally, thank you Karma. You were my best friend and the greatest companion a man could ask for. Not a single day passes without me thinking of the love and grace you shared with the world.

I would also like to recognize everyone else who is not mentioned in my acknowledgments section for all their contributions to make this book a reality.

A.C. Burton
Angelita Almedia
Ashley Steffes
Barkha Daily
Brian Huibregtse
Bryan Henslin
Cari Lynn McLean
Cesar Salinas
Chris Li
Colin Kaepernick
Courtney Eder
Courtney Strauer
Charles Monroe-Kane
Chuck Oexmann
Danielle Schwendimann
David Feehan
Dr. Brandon Kooi
Dr. Lauren Seiter
Elena Runge

Emily Killeen
Eric Koester
Gabe & Hallah Nunez
Gabe & Lisa Nunez
Ibram X. Kendi
Ish Harris
Jackie Koepke
Jae Edwards
Jamie Calloway
Jason Huibregtse
Jen Cousineau
Jennifer Peltz
Jeremy Cumberland
Jesse Wendorf
Joann H. Feehan
Joel Mathwig
Joshua Boyd
Joshua Willmann
Judith Sackett

Justin Fons
Katherine Garcia
Katie Trew Atkinson
Katrina Mayer
Keri Kaun
Krista Mallas
Kristina Bauer
Kyle Sackett
Lacey Sadoff
Lindsey Kaiser
Lyndsey Hustad
Mary Jane Almeida
Melinda & Reynaldo Angel
Mike & Heather Nunez
Morgan Haili Jacek
Peggy Masterson Hahn

Petra Ostman
Priscilla Nunez
Roxanne Staehler
Sadie Villegas
Sara Stoinski
Shelly Dutch
Skye Boughman
Steffanni LaJeunesse
Tanya Thompson Kehoe
Theresa Alexander
Thomas Ernest
Tim Ryan
Toni Falligant
Trisha Berger
Victoria Nunez
Xavier Moreno

APPENDIX

———

CHAPTER 8

Brooks, Rosa. "Stop Training Police Like They're Joining the Military." *The Atlantic*, June 10, 2020. *https://www.theatlantic.com/ideas/archive/2020/06/police-academies-paramilitary/612859/.*

Edwards, Frank, Lee, Hedwig, Esposito, Michael. "Risk of being killed by police use of force in the United States by age, race–ethnicity, and sex." *Proceedings of the National Academy of Sciences,* 116 no. 34 (Aug 2019):16793-16798. DOI: 10.1073/pnas.1821204116.

CHAPTER 11

Charles Tubbs's LinkedIn Page. Accessed June 10, 2021. *https://www.linkedin.com/in/charles-a-tubbs-sr-42541620/.*

CHAPTER 21

US Census Bureau. "QuickFacts Dane County, WI." *https://www.census.gov/quickfacts/danecountywisconsin.*

CHAPTER 28

Bell, Diane. "Stolen art in Wisconsin has link to San Diego." *Hartford Courant,* Accessed February 19, 2016. *https://www.courant. com/sdut-aaron-bohrod-painting-faulconer-gloria-ted-talk-2016feb19-story.html.*

54456402R00125